UNIVERSE UNLOCKED

A KID'S GUIDE TO THE STARS AND BEYOND

BRIAN THOMAS

Copyright © 2024 by Brian Thomas

All rights reserved.

No part of this book may be reproduced in any form or by any electronic or mechanical means, including information storage and retrieval systems, without written permission from the author, except for the use of brief quotations in a book review.

1
WHAT IS ASTRONOMY?

Astronomy might sound like a big, fancy word, but at its heart, it's all about curiosity. Humans have always looked up and wondered, "What's out there?" Thousands of years ago, people noticed that some stars formed patterns, which we call constellations today. They noticed that certain bright lights moved differently across the sky—those turned out to be planets. And over time, people built telescopes, flew rockets, and even sent astronauts into space to get closer to the things we could only see from a distance. Astronomy is like the ultimate detective work of the universe. Instead of finding clues on the ground, astronomers look for clues in the sky.

One of the coolest things about astronomy is that it covers a lot of ground—or rather, a lot of space! When astronomers study the stars, they're learning about giant, burning balls of gas, some of which are many times bigger than our Sun. There are different kinds of stars out there—some are small and burn very brightly, while others are enormous but are so far away that they look tiny to us. Stars also have their own life cycles. They're born, they burn brightly, and eventually, they "die" in spectacular explosions known as supernovas. These explosions are so powerful that they create new elements, like the ones we find here on Earth!

Beyond stars, astronomers study planets. Some planets, like Mars, are rocky and have surfaces that we could imagine landing on. Others, like Jupiter, are made of gas and don't have solid ground. Each planet has its own set of mysteries. For example, why is Mars so red? (Hint: it's because of iron oxide, which is basically rust!) Why does Jupiter have a massive storm, called the Great Red Spot, that's been raging for centuries? And then there's Earth, the only planet we know of so far that has life. Studying planets helps astronomers understand not only how planets work but also how Earth fits into the bigger picture of space.

Astronomers also look at galaxies, which are huge collections of stars, planets, gas, and dust, all held together by gravity. Our galaxy, the Milky Way, has billions of stars in it, including our Sun. Just think about that for a moment: billions of stars! And the Milky Way is only one galaxy among many; in fact, there are billions of galaxies out there, each one with its own stars, planets, and mysteries. Some galaxies even collide with each other, creating massive cosmic fireworks. By studying galaxies, astronomers try to learn more about how the universe itself began and how it might change over time.

In addition to stars, planets, and galaxies, astronomers study smaller objects like asteroids and comets. Asteroids are rocky objects that orbit the Sun, mostly found in a region called the asteroid belt between Mars and Jupiter. Comets are different; they're made of ice, dust, and rock. When a comet gets close to the Sun, it starts to heat up, creating a glowing tail that can stretch for thousands of miles. Some people call comets "dirty snowballs" because of their icy makeup. These objects might be small, but they can give us big clues about what our solar system was like billions of years ago.

One amazing thing about astronomy is that it combines a lot of different sciences. There's physics, which helps explain how things like gravity work in space. There's chemistry, which tells us about the elements that make up stars, planets, and even the air we breathe on Earth. And there's even geology, which is the study of rocks, used to study rocky planets like Mars. Astronomers are like detectives, using all these sciences to answer questions about the universe. They look at how planets orbit the Sun, how stars form and explode, and how galaxies move in space.

If you've ever heard of the "Big Bang," that's one of

the biggest questions in astronomy. The Big Bang is the theory that the universe started with a huge explosion about 13.8 billion years ago. Before that, there was nothing—not even time or space! This massive explosion created everything we see today: stars, planets, galaxies, and even the space between them. Since the Big Bang, the universe has been expanding, and astronomers are still trying to understand exactly why it's expanding and what that means for the future.

Now, you might wonder how astronomers can know so much about things that are so far away. After all, you can't exactly pick up a star or a galaxy and study it in a lab! Instead, astronomers use telescopes and other special tools to gather clues. Telescopes let us see objects that are incredibly far away, even things that are millions or billions of light-years from Earth. And "light-year" is another interesting concept—it's the distance that light travels in one year. Light is the fastest thing we know of, so just imagine how big a distance a light-year is!

Astronomers use all kinds of telescopes. Some are on the ground, like the giant telescopes in Hawaii that let astronomers see objects very clearly. Others are in space, like the Hubble Space Telescope, which has been sending back amazing images of galaxies, stars, and planets since 1990. The reason we put telescopes in space is to get a clearer view; the Earth's atmosphere can make distant objects look blurry, but space telescopes don't have that problem.

Why Astronomy Matters

Why do people spend so much time, money, and energy exploring the universe? Why do astronomers spend years studying stars, galaxies, and planets? You might wonder why astronomy really matters. After all, we live here on Earth. Why focus so much on what's out there in space? Well, it turns out that understanding the universe actually helps us understand a lot about ourselves and our place in it. In other words, studying the universe reminds us that we're part of something much bigger.

Let's start with Earth itself. Every day, we rely on things like the Sun for warmth and light, or the Moon for ocean tides. These are cosmic forces that affect us all the time, even though we might not notice it. If you think about it, astronomy is woven into our lives in all kinds of ways. The Sun, for instance, isn't just a big light bulb in the sky. It's a giant ball of burning gas, and without it, life on Earth wouldn't be possible. In fact, all life on Earth depends on energy from the Sun. Plants use sunlight to grow, and animals, including humans, rely on plants or other animals that eat plants. The Sun isn't just another star out there in space; it's our star, the one that makes life possible. Understanding how the Sun works helps us understand how other stars work, too, and even how life might exist on planets that orbit other stars.

Then there's the Moon, Earth's closest neighbor.

For thousands of years, humans have been fascinated by the Moon, using it to track time, plan farming, and even inspire myths and legends. The Moon's gravity pulls on Earth's oceans, creating tides that help shape our coastlines and influence marine life. By studying the Moon, we've learned about its surface, its craters, and even its history – it was once a part of Earth, separated after a massive collision billions of years ago. When astronauts landed on the Moon, they didn't just bring back rocks; they brought back knowledge. They helped us understand more about Earth's history, too. The Moon is like a little piece of Earth's story.

Now, let's think even bigger. Earth isn't alone in space – we're part of a solar system, a family of planets orbiting the Sun. Each planet is unique, with its own set of features. For instance, Mars is covered in rust-colored dust and has huge volcanoes. Jupiter is a gas giant with a storm larger than Earth that's been raging for centuries. Studying these planets gives us clues about what makes Earth special. For example, we know that Mars once had rivers and lakes, but today it's a cold desert. By studying Mars, we learn more about climate change and how planets can change over time. This knowledge might even help us understand and protect Earth's environment.

But our solar system is just one part of an even bigger system – the galaxy. Our galaxy, the Milky Way, has billions of stars, each with the potential to have planets orbiting them. Some of these planets might even have the right conditions for life. Imagine that: somewhere out there, in the vastness of space, there could be other planets with oceans, clouds, and maybe even creatures. This is one of the big reasons astronomers study the stars and galaxies – to learn more about our place in the universe. Are we alone, or are there other forms of life out there? Finding the answer to that question could change the way we see ourselves and our world.

Astronomy also teaches us about time itself. When we look up at the stars, we're actually looking back in time. Light takes time to travel across space, and some of the stars we see are so far away that their light has taken millions of years to reach us. This means that when we look at a distant star, we're seeing it as it was millions of years ago. Some of those stars might not even exist anymore! They might have exploded in a supernova, leaving behind only a memory in the form of starlight. Astronomy is like a time machine, letting us peek into the past of our universe.

And then there's the question of the beginning of everything. Astronomers believe that the universe began with a massive explosion called the Big Bang about 13.8 billion years ago. Everything we see – stars, planets, galaxies – all came from this single, incredibly hot point. By studying the universe, astronomers are trying to understand how it all started and how it has changed over billions of years. Learning about the Big Bang is a way of learning about our own origins. It's mind-boggling to think that every atom in our bodies, every bit of matter, was created in that early universe.

Astronomy also gives us a sense of connection. The elements that make up stars – like hydrogen and helium – are also found in our own bodies. In fact, most of the elements that make up everything on Earth, including you and me, were created inside stars that exploded billions of years ago. This means that we're literally made of stardust! When you look up at the stars, you're not just looking at distant objects; you're looking at something that's part of your own story. Astronomy helps us see that we're connected to the universe in ways we might not have realized.

As if that weren't enough, studying astronomy also helps us protect our planet. By learning about asteroids, comets, and other space objects, astronomers help keep Earth safe from potential dangers. For instance, astronomers track the paths of asteroids to make sure they won't collide with Earth. If a large asteroid were to hit our planet, it could cause serious damage, like the one that scientists think wiped out the dinosaurs. By keeping an eye on space, astronomers can give us early warnings and even help develop plans to avoid future collisions.

And who knows? One day, humans might travel to other planets. Astronomy is already helping us prepare for that. Scientists are studying places like Mars and the Moon to see if humans could live there. They're looking at ways to grow food in space, recycle water, and build shelters. By exploring these ideas, astronomers and scientists are taking the first steps toward a future where humans could live on other planets. Imagine what it would be like to have people living on Mars or even further out in the galaxy!

There's a lot of mystery out there, too. Dark matter, dark energy, black holes – these are things that astronomers are still trying to understand. We know dark matter exists because we can see its effects on galaxies, but we don't know exactly what it is. Dark energy seems to be causing the universe to expand faster and faster, but again, it's still a big mystery. Black holes are so powerful that not even light can escape from them. Studying these strange phenomena helps us understand the laws of physics in extreme conditions. These mysteries remind us that there's always more to learn, no matter how much we think we know.

A Brief History

Thousands of years ago, in places like ancient Egypt, China, Mesopotamia, and Greece, people looked to the stars for guidance. In ancient Egypt, people noticed that the flooding of the Nile River, which they depended on to grow crops, happened around the same time each year when a bright star appeared in the sky. This star was Sirius, and its rising just before sunrise marked the start of the flood season. The Egyptians were paying close attention to the stars because it helped them survive. They even built huge structures, like the pyramids, with certain stars in mind, lining up the pyramids with specific points in the sky. For them, astronomy was a way to understand the cycles of nature.

In ancient China, astronomers took careful note of the patterns in the sky as well. They were some of the first to record events like solar and lunar eclipses, which were rare and impressive sights. They noticed how the Moon sometimes blocked the Sun or how the shadow of the Earth would cross over the Moon, turning it dark. These events seemed powerful and mysterious, and Chinese astronomers wanted to predict when they would happen. They kept detailed records of these events, which helped later generations understand the movements of the Sun, Earth, and Moon.

The Greeks had their own ideas about the stars and planets, too. One of the most famous ancient Greek astronomers, Ptolemy, came up with a model of the universe where he imagined Earth was at the center. He thought all the planets, the Sun, and the stars revolved around Earth in a perfect, circular path. This idea made sense to people at the time, because from where we stand on Earth, it feels like we're at the center of everything. The stars look like they're moving across the sky, but it's really Earth rotating. Ptolemy's ideas were accepted for over a thousand years because no one had a better way to explain what they saw – yet.

While the Greeks were theorizing, ancient people in other parts of the world, like the Mayans in Central America, were also developing impressive astronomical knowledge. The Mayans built large stone structures and observed the sky to keep track of time. They created detailed calendars based on the movements of the Sun, the Moon, and the stars. Their calendar was so accurate that it could predict solar and lunar events hundreds of years into the future! To the Mayans, astronomy wasn't just a science – it was connected to their religion, daily life, and even their understanding of time.

Then, as centuries passed, new ideas began to challenge the old beliefs. During the Renaissance, a period in Europe known for its explosion of art, science, and learning, people started to question the idea that Earth was at the center of the universe. A Polish astronomer named Nicolaus Copernicus came up with a revolutionary idea: what if the Sun, not Earth, was at the center? He suggested that Earth and the other planets actually revolved around the Sun. This was a bold idea because it went against everything people had believed for centuries, but it helped explain why planets sometimes appeared to move backward in the sky, something the old Earth-centered model struggled to explain.

After Copernicus, a scientist named Galileo Galilei

made more groundbreaking discoveries. Galileo was one of the first people to use a telescope to study the sky. This might sound simple, but at the time, it was a huge deal! With his telescope, Galileo could see things no one else had ever seen. He discovered that Jupiter had moons orbiting around it, which showed that not everything in space revolved around Earth. He also observed the phases of Venus, which supported Copernicus's idea that planets orbit the Sun. Galileo's discoveries changed the way people thought about the universe, but they also got him into trouble with leaders who didn't like the idea of challenging long-held beliefs.

Another astronomer who changed everything was Johannes Kepler. He studied the way planets move and realized that their orbits weren't perfect circles, like people had thought, but ellipses – kind of like squashed circles. This discovery helped explain why planets moved faster when they were closer to the Sun and slower when they were farther away. Kepler's work built a foundation for modern astronomy, showing that the universe followed certain laws that could be measured and predicted.

Then came Isaac Newton, who figured out one of the biggest mysteries of all: gravity. He realized that gravity was the force keeping planets in orbit around the Sun, moons around planets, and even us anchored to the ground on Earth. Newton's law of gravity helped explain the movements of the stars, planets, and galaxies, making it clear that the universe wasn't just random. There were patterns, rules, and forces that held everything together.

In the 20th century, astronomy took an even bigger leap forward with the work of people like Albert Einstein. He proposed that space and time were connected in something called "space-time" and that massive objects, like stars and planets, could bend space-time, causing the force we feel as gravity. His ideas were strange and complex, but they helped astronomers understand things like black holes, which are regions in space where gravity is so strong that nothing, not even light, can escape.

As technology advanced, astronomers began to send telescopes into space. The Hubble Space Telescope, launched in 1990, was able to capture images of galaxies billions of light-years away, giving us a glimpse of the universe's early history. With the Hubble, scientists discovered that the universe is expanding – galaxies are moving away from each other, like spots on a balloon that's being blown up. This discovery led to the theory of the Big Bang, the idea that the universe began as a single, incredibly dense point that exploded outward.

Today, astronomers continue to make amazing discoveries. With tools like radio telescopes, space probes, and even robotic explorers on Mars, they are uncovering new secrets about our universe all the time. We now know that there are billions of galaxies, each with billions of stars. Some of those stars have planets that might be a lot like Earth, which makes us wonder if life could exist elsewhere in the universe. Astronomy has come a long way from the days when people thought the Earth was the center of everything.

2

OUR SOLAR SYSTEM

The Sun

The Sun is a star, just like the countless others we see in the night sky, but it's much closer to us. In fact, the Sun is about 93 million miles away from Earth. This distance might sound enormous, but for space, that's actually quite close! Because the Sun is so much closer to us than other stars, it looks much larger and brighter than anything else in the sky. If we were to travel that distance, it would take us years with today's fastest spacecraft, but thankfully, the Sun's light reaches us much faster. Light from the Sun takes just over eight minutes to travel to Earth, which is pretty amazing when you think about how far away it is.

But what exactly is the Sun made of? The Sun is a

massive, burning ball of gas, mainly made up of hydrogen and helium. Imagine a fire so big that it's about 109 times the diameter of Earth! The Sun's surface, which we can see, is called the photosphere, and it's incredibly hot – around 10,000 degrees Fahrenheit. But the real heat is at its core, deep inside the Sun, where temperatures reach about 27 million degrees Fahrenheit. This is where something incredible happens: nuclear fusion.

Nuclear fusion is a process that powers the Sun. It's like a giant engine, where hydrogen atoms collide with each other at high speeds and temperatures, fusing together to form helium. Every time this fusion happens, it releases a huge amount of energy in the form of light and heat. This energy travels outward through layers of the Sun and eventually reaches us here on Earth as sunlight. The Sun's energy is so powerful that it's been shining for over 4.5 billion years, and it has enough fuel to keep shining for several billion more.

One of the amazing things about the Sun's energy is that it doesn't just give us light and warmth. It also fuels life itself. Plants, for example, use sunlight to make their own food through a process called photosynthesis. During photosynthesis, plants absorb sunlight and turn it into energy they can use to grow. This process also produces oxygen, which is what we breathe. When animals, including humans, eat plants, they're also consuming that stored energy from the Sun. In this way, the Sun is at the very beginning of almost every food chain on Earth.

Besides providing energy, the Sun also helps keep our planet's climate stable. As Earth orbits around the Sun, it receives a certain amount of heat, which keeps our planet warm enough for water to stay in liquid form. Water is essential for all living things, and Earth's temperature is just right for it – thanks to the Sun. If Earth were any closer, it would be too hot, and if it were any farther away, it would be too cold. This is sometimes called the "Goldilocks Zone," because it's "just right" for life as we know it. And Earth isn't the only planet in our solar system that orbits the Sun; each planet moves in its own path, held in place by the Sun's gravity.

Gravity is one of the most important forces in the universe, and it's what keeps everything in the solar system connected to the Sun. You can think of gravity as an invisible rope that pulls objects toward each other. The Sun's gravity is incredibly strong because the Sun is so massive. Its gravity is what keeps Earth, the Moon, and all the other planets in orbit. Without this gravitational pull, Earth would just float off into space. The Sun's gravity is like the glue holding our solar system together, ensuring that each planet stays in its place.

Sometimes, the Sun isn't just a peaceful source of

light and warmth. It also has its wild side. The Sun has spots on its surface, called sunspots, which are cooler areas that appear darker than the rest of the Sun. These sunspots are caused by intense magnetic activity. Every now and then, the Sun releases bursts of energy in the form of solar flares or coronal mass ejections (CMEs). These are powerful explosions that send streams of charged particles flying through space. When these particles reach Earth, they can cause a display of colorful lights in the sky called the auroras – the Northern Lights and Southern Lights. They can also interfere with satellite signals and even affect our electricity grids here on Earth.

The Sun might seem like it's always the same, but it actually goes through its own cycles. Every 11 years or so, the Sun goes through what scientists call the solar cycle. During this cycle, the number of sunspots and solar flares increases and decreases. When the Sun is at the peak of its cycle, we see more sunspots and solar activity. This cycle affects the space environment around Earth, which is why scientists study it closely. Understanding the Sun's behavior helps us predict things like solar storms, which can affect our technology on Earth.

Even though the Sun feels permanent, it won't shine forever. Like all stars, the Sun has a life cycle. Right now, it's in the middle of its life, and it's stable. But eventually, billions of years from now, the Sun will run out of hydrogen to burn. When that happens, it will start to change. It will grow larger, becoming a red giant, and it will expand so much that it could swallow up the inner planets, possibly including Earth. After that, the Sun will shed its outer layers, leaving behind a small, hot core called a white dwarf. This will be the final stage of the Sun's life, and it will slowly cool down over billions of years until it no longer shines.

It might sound a little sad that the Sun won't last forever, but there's no need to worry. The Sun still has billions of years left, which is more than enough time for us to keep exploring, discovering, and learning about our solar system. The Sun's life cycle is a reminder that even the most powerful things in the universe go through changes. Just like people and planets, stars have a beginning, a middle, and an end.

Planets of the Solar System

Mercury: The Speedy One

First up is Mercury, the closest planet to the Sun. Mercury is a small planet, not much bigger than our Moon, but it's fast – incredibly fast. It zips around the Sun faster than any other planet in our solar system, completing a full orbit in just 88 days! That's less than three months, so a year on Mercury goes by in the blink of an eye. But here's something surprising: even though Mercury is close to the Sun, it's not the hottest planet. This tiny planet has almost no atmosphere to trap heat, which means that at night, it gets super cold, reaching temperatures way below freezing. During the day, though, Mercury's surface heats up to a scorching 800 degrees Fahrenheit.

Venus: Earth's Fiery Twin

Next, we have Venus, which is often called Earth's "twin" because it's similar in size and structure. But that's where the similarities end. Venus is the hottest planet in the solar system, with surface temperatures that can melt lead. Its thick, toxic atmosphere is full of clouds made from sulfuric acid, which traps heat like a blanket in a process called the greenhouse effect. Venus's atmosphere is so thick that it creates crushing pressure on the surface. If you stood on Venus (which you wouldn't want to!), it would feel like being under an ocean on Earth. And here's a weird fact: a day on Venus is longer than a year! Venus takes about 243 Earth days to complete a single rotation on its axis, but it orbits the Sun in only 225 days.

Earth: The Only One with Life

Now we come to our home, Earth. Earth is the only planet we know of that has life, and it's also the only one with liquid water on its surface. About 70% of Earth is covered in oceans, rivers, and lakes, which makes it a "blue planet." Earth has the perfect conditions for life, thanks to its distance from the Sun, which keeps it not too hot and not too cold. It also has a protective atmosphere that shields us from harmful space radiation and a magnetic field that deflects the solar wind. Earth has one moon, which influences our ocean tides and has been a big part of human culture and history for thousands of years.

Mars: The Red Planet

Moving on, we come to Mars, often called the Red Planet because of its rusty color. This color comes from iron oxide, or rust, in its soil. Mars is one of the most explored planets in our solar system, with rovers like Curiosity and Perseverance exploring its surface. Mars has mountains, valleys, and even the largest volcano in the solar system, Olympus Mons, which is about three times taller than Mount Everest! Mars is a cold desert world, with temperatures that can drop to -80 degrees Fahrenheit at night. Scientists are particularly interested in Mars because it once had rivers, lakes, and possibly even oceans. This makes it a prime candidate in the search for past life in our solar system.

Jupiter: The Giant of the Solar System

Next, we arrive at Jupiter, the largest planet in the solar system. Jupiter is a gas giant, which means it's made mostly of hydrogen and helium, like a mini-Sun. You wouldn't be able to stand on Jupiter's surface, because it doesn't have a solid one! Jupiter is famous for its Great Red Spot, a massive storm that has been raging for at least 300 years. This storm is so big that you could fit two Earths inside it. Jupiter also has the most moons of any planet in our solar system, with more than 75 discovered so far. Some of its largest moons, like Europa and Ganymede, have icy surfaces and might even have oceans beneath, which makes scientists curious about the possibility of life there.

Saturn: The Ringed Beauty

Beyond Jupiter, we find Saturn, the planet famous for its stunning rings. Saturn's rings are made of billions of tiny ice and rock particles, ranging in size from specks of dust to chunks as big as a house. No other planet has rings quite like Saturn's, which are wide and bright enough to see with a telescope from Earth. Saturn is also a gas giant, and it's almost as large as Jupiter, though much lighter. It's a very windy place, with winds reaching over 1,000 miles per hour near the equator. Saturn has more than 80 moons, with Titan being the largest. Titan is especially interesting because it has rivers and lakes – not of water, but of liquid methane!

Uranus: The Tilted Planet

After Saturn comes Uranus, a planet that's famous for being tipped on its side. While most planets spin upright or slightly tilted, Uranus rotates almost completely sideways, with its poles facing where other planets have their equators. This unique tilt likely happened because Uranus was hit by a large object early in its history. Uranus is a blue-green color due to the methane in its atmosphere, which absorbs red light and reflects blue. It's an "ice giant," meaning it's made of icy materials like water, ammonia, and methane, along with hydrogen and helium. And while Uranus doesn't have rings as visible as Saturn's, it does have faint rings that were only discovered recently.

Neptune: The Windy Blue World

Last but not least, we reach Neptune, the farthest planet from the Sun. Neptune is another ice giant, similar in size and composition to Uranus, and it's a beautiful deep blue color. Neptune is known for having the strongest winds in the solar system, with speeds that reach up to 1,200 miles per hour – that's faster than the speed of sound! Neptune also has a large storm system, similar to Jupiter's Great Red Spot, called the Great Dark Spot. This storm was discovered by the Voyager 2 spacecraft in 1989 but has since disappeared, showing that Neptune's storms can come and go. Neptune has 14 known moons, with Triton being the largest. Triton is one of the coldest places in the solar system and has geysers that spew icy particles.

The Dwarf Planets

Beyond Neptune, there are other objects that don't quite fit the definition of a planet. These are the dwarf planets, like Pluto, which was once considered the ninth planet. In 2006, astronomers reclassified Pluto as a dwarf planet because it shares its space with other objects in the Kuiper Belt, a region filled with icy bodies. Pluto is still a fascinating world, though, with mountains made of ice, a thin atmosphere, and even a heart-shaped glacier on its surface. Other dwarf planets in our solar system include Eris, Haumea, and Makemake, each with their own unique features and mysteries.

Moons, Asteroids, and Comets

Moons: Our Companions in Orbit

Moons are one of the most fascinating parts of our solar system. A moon is a natural satellite, meaning it's a smaller body that orbits a planet. Earth has only one moon, which we simply call "the Moon," but many other planets have multiple moons, each with its own character and story.

Jupiter, for instance, has more than 75 moons! Four of them – Io, Europa, Ganymede, and Callisto – are called the Galilean moons, named after the astronomer Galileo who first spotted them through a telescope in 1610. These moons are each like miniature worlds. Io is covered in active volcanoes, constantly erupting and reshaping its surface. Europa is an icy moon with a smooth, shiny surface, and scientists believe it might have an ocean of liquid water beneath its icy crust. Ganymede is the largest moon in the solar system, even bigger than the planet Mercury! It has a magnetic field, something unusual for a moon. Callisto is covered with craters from impacts over billions of years, showing its long history.

Saturn's moon Titan is another standout. Titan has a thick atmosphere and lakes of liquid methane, a substance similar to natural gas here on Earth. This orange-tinged moon has rivers, lakes, and even weather patterns, but instead of water, it's liquid methane that flows and evaporates. Another of Saturn's moons, Enceladus, has geysers that shoot water ice into space, suggesting that there's a salty ocean beneath its icy surface. The Cassini spacecraft even flew through these icy plumes and detected hints of organic molecules, the building blocks of life!

Mars has two tiny, oddly shaped moons, Phobos and Deimos. These little moons look more like potatoes than the round moons we might imagine. Scientists think they may have once been asteroids that got caught by Mars's gravity. Phobos, the larger of the two, is slowly being pulled toward Mars and may eventually crash into the planet or break apart to form a ring. Each moon in our solar system has its own quirks, and they remind us that moons can come in all shapes, sizes, and types.

Asteroids: Space Rocks with a Story

Asteroids are rocky objects that orbit the Sun, mainly found in a region between Mars and Jupiter called the asteroid belt. This belt is like a crowded highway of space rocks, with asteroids of all shapes and sizes. Some are as small as pebbles, while others are hundreds of miles wide. Asteroids are made from materials left over from the formation of the solar system, so they're like time capsules, giving us a peek into the past.

One of the largest asteroids in the asteroid belt is Ceres. It's so big that it's also classified as a dwarf planet. Ceres has its own mysteries – recent space missions have found that it has bright spots on its surface, which are thought to be salty deposits, possibly from ice or water that once flowed there. Other well-known asteroids include Vesta, which has a massive mountain nearly twice the height of Mount Everest, and Pallas, which has a slightly tilted orbit compared to most objects in the asteroid belt.

Sometimes, asteroids don't stay in the asteroid belt. They can get pulled out of their orbits by the gravity of planets, especially by the giant Jupiter, and head off on new paths through the solar system. Occasionally, asteroids can come close to Earth, and while most are harmless, scientists keep an eye on them. In fact, there are special observatories and even space missions dedicated to tracking asteroids that could pose a risk to Earth. One of these missions, called OSIRIS-REx, recently collected a sample from an asteroid named Bennu and brought it back to Earth to study. These samples will help us understand more about what asteroids are made of and how they might have delivered essential materials to Earth long ago.

Comets: Cosmic Snowballs with Tails

Comets are often described as "dirty snowballs" because they're made of ice, dust, and rocky material. Comets originate from the colder, outer parts of the solar system, and they spend most of their time far from the Sun. But when a comet gets closer to the Sun, its icy surface starts to heat up and turn into gas. This process creates a glowing "coma," or cloud, around the comet's center, and a bright tail that streams out behind it.

There are two main regions in our solar system where comets come from: the Kuiper Belt and the Oort Cloud. The Kuiper Belt is a ring of icy bodies beyond Neptune, where you'll find dwarf planets like Pluto and many comets that have shorter orbits around the Sun. The Oort Cloud is much farther away, a distant cloud of icy objects surrounding the solar system, where long-period comets come from. These comets take hundreds or even thousands of years to complete one orbit.

One of the most famous comets is Halley's Comet. It's a "short-period" comet, which means it visits the inner solar system relatively often – about every 76 years. People have been observing Halley's Comet for centuries, and it was last visible from Earth in 1986. Halley's Comet will make its next appearance in 2061, so it's a rare sight that happens only once in a lifetime for most people.

Comets have often been seen as omens or symbols of change throughout history. Before people understood what they were, comets were mysterious visitors in the night sky. Today, scientists study comets to learn more about the early solar system. Since comets are made of ancient ice and dust, they hold clues about what conditions were like billions of years ago. In 2014, a spacecraft called Rosetta became the first mission to orbit a comet, 67P/Churyumov-Gerasimenko, and even sent a lander named Philae to its surface. Rosetta's mission helped scientists learn more about the composition of comets and how they behave as they move closer to the Sun.

Meteoroids, Meteors, and Meteorites: Space Rocks That Come to Us

Sometimes, small pieces of asteroids or comets break off and start traveling through space. These smaller pieces are called meteoroids. When a meteoroid enters Earth's atmosphere, it burns up due to friction with the air, creating a bright streak of light known as a meteor – or what many people call a "shooting star." If you've ever made a wish on a shooting star, you were actually wishing on a meteor.

Occasionally, a meteoroid is large enough that it doesn't completely burn up in the atmosphere and lands on Earth's surface. When this happens, it's called a meteorite. Meteorites can range in size from tiny specks to massive boulders. Some meteorites are made of rock, while others are made of metal, and a few are a mix of both. Each meteorite that lands on Earth brings with it information about space and the early solar system. Scientists study them to learn more about the types of materials that were around when the planets were forming.

One famous meteorite impact happened about

50,000 years ago in what is now Arizona, creating the Barringer Crater. This crater is over a mile wide and 550 feet deep, formed by a meteorite that was probably about 150 feet across. Large impacts like this are rare, but they show just how powerful even small objects from space can be.

3

STARS, CONSTELLATIONS, AND GALAXIES

What are Stars?

Stars begin their lives in giant clouds of gas and dust floating through space, often called nebulae. A nebula is like a cosmic nursery where stars are born. These clouds are mostly made of hydrogen, the simplest and most common element in the universe. But even though hydrogen is simple, it's incredibly powerful when it comes to forming stars. Inside a nebula, gravity starts to pull the gas and dust together, forming clumps. As these clumps get denser, they start to collapse under their own gravity, creating what scientists call a protostar.

As the protostar forms, it heats up. All the gas and dust collapsing in on itself creates an intense pressure, which causes the temperature at the center of the protostar to rise. When it gets hot enough—around 15 million degrees Celsius—something amazing happens: nuclear fusion begins. This is the process that will power the star for most of its life. During fusion, hydrogen atoms collide with each other and fuse to form helium, releasing a huge amount of energy in the process. This energy is what makes stars shine. Once fusion starts, the protostar has officially become a star.

Now that the star is shining, it enters the main phase of its life, known as the "main sequence." During this stage, the star is stable, with the force of gravity pulling inward balanced by the outward pressure from nuclear fusion. For most stars, this main sequence phase is the longest part of their lives. Our own Sun, for example, is currently in its main sequence and has been for about 4.5 billion years. It's expected to stay in this phase for another 5 billion years or so. Stars in this stage can vary in size, temperature, and color. The hottest stars are blue and white, while cooler stars are yellow, orange, or red. A star's color depends on its temperature, with blue being the hottest and red being the coolest.

Eventually, however, a star runs out of hydrogen to fuse. When this happens, the star's life begins to change dramatically. If the star is similar in size to our Sun, it will swell up into a red giant. As it expands, the outer layers of the star cool down, giving it a reddish color. Inside, however, the star's core is heating up even more. With hydrogen running out, the star begins to fuse helium into heavier elements, like carbon and oxygen. This fusion process doesn't last as long as the hydrogen fusion, and the star becomes increasingly unstable.

As the red giant phase ends, the outer layers of the star drift away, creating a beautiful shell of gas around the core, called a planetary nebula. What's left at the center is a small, dense core, known as a white dwarf. A white dwarf is about the size of Earth but incredibly dense—just a teaspoon of white dwarf material would weigh tons! Over time, the white dwarf cools and fades, eventually becoming a cold, dark "black dwarf." However, this process takes billions of years, so there probably aren't any black dwarfs in the universe yet since it hasn't existed long enough for a white dwarf to cool that much.

The life cycle of a massive star—the kind that's much bigger than our Sun—is even more dramatic. Like smaller stars, massive stars also spend a long time in the main sequence, fusing hydrogen into helium. But because they're so large, they burn through their hydrogen much faster and move on to the next stages more quickly. When a massive star exhausts its hydrogen, it too swells up, but instead of becoming a red giant, it becomes a red supergiant. These stars are enormous, with some supergiants being hundreds or even thousands of times the size of our Sun.

Inside a supergiant, fusion continues, producing heavier and heavier elements. After helium, it fuses carbon, then oxygen, and so on, all the way up to iron. But iron is different from the other elements. Fusing iron doesn't release energy; instead, it absorbs it. This is a problem for the star because fusion is what has been keeping the star stable against gravity. When iron builds up in the core, the star can no longer produce enough energy to counteract the force of gravity. Eventually, gravity wins, and the core collapses in a fraction of a second.

This sudden collapse causes one of the most powerful explosions in the universe: a supernova. In a supernova, the outer layers of the star are blasted into space, creating a burst of light and energy that can outshine entire galaxies for a short time. The explosion is so powerful that it creates elements heavier than iron, like gold and uranium, which are then scattered across the universe. These elements eventually become part of new stars, planets, and even life forms. In fact, many of the atoms in your body were formed in the cores of stars or in supernova explosions billions of years ago.

After a supernova, what's left of the star's core depends on how massive it was. If the core is relatively small, it will become a neutron star. A neutron star is incredibly dense – just a sugar-cube-sized amount of neutron star material would weigh about as much as all of humanity! Neutron stars also have intense magnetic fields and can spin very rapidly. Some neutron stars emit beams of radiation from their poles, and when these beams sweep past Earth, we see them as flashes of light. These flashing neutron stars are called pulsars.

But if the star was exceptionally massive, even a neutron star can't hold up against the force of gravity. In this case, the core collapses further to form a black hole. A black hole is a region of space where gravity is so strong that not even light can escape from it. Black holes are some of the most mysterious objects in the universe, and scientists are still studying them to understand what happens inside them. Once a star becomes a black hole, it's essentially the end of its life cycle, although it can continue to affect the space around it by pulling in nearby stars and gas with its immense gravity.

The life cycle of a star is a reminder that nothing in the universe lasts forever. Stars are born, they shine brightly for millions or billions of years, and eventually, they reach an end. But even in death, stars continue to play a role in the universe. Supernovas scatter elements that become part of new stars and planets, and even black holes and neutron stars add their own unique energy and mystery to the cosmos.

Constellations

The Big Dipper and Ursa Major: The Great Bear

One of the first star patterns you might recognize is the Big Dipper. It's an easy one to find because it has a distinct shape, like a ladle or a big spoon. But did you know that the Big Dipper is actually part of a larger constellation called Ursa Major, or the Great Bear? Imagine a giant bear in the sky, with the Big Dipper as part of its back and tail.

The story of the Great Bear comes from Greek mythology. According to one legend, Zeus, the king of the gods, fell in love with a woman named Callisto, who was very beautiful. This made Zeus's wife, Hera, jealous. To punish Callisto, Hera turned her into a bear. For many years, Callisto roamed the forest as a bear, until one day she crossed paths with her own son, Arcas. Not recognizing his mother, Arcas was about to hunt her, but Zeus intervened. To save them, he turned both Callisto and Arcas into constellations, placing them in the sky as Ursa Major, the Great Bear, and Ursa Minor, the Little Bear. That's why the stars in these constellations seem to circle the North Star, Polaris, which is located in the Little Bear.

Orion: The Mighty Hunter

Orion is another constellation with a fascinating story and one of the easiest to spot. It has a distinct shape, with three bright stars in a row forming "Orion's Belt." Orion also has two bright stars on either side, Betelgeuse and Rigel, which mark his shoulders and feet. With a little imagination, the whole constellation looks like a person standing with a bow and arrow, ready for the hunt.

In Greek mythology, Orion was a mighty hunter

and one of the few mortals who could match the gods in bravery and strength. He was a close friend of the goddess Artemis, who was also a hunter. But Orion was boastful and claimed he could hunt down every animal on Earth. This angered Gaia, the goddess of the Earth, who sent a giant scorpion to stop him. In the end, the scorpion stung Orion, and he died. To honor him, the gods placed him in the sky as a constellation. The Scorpius constellation, representing the scorpion, was also placed in the sky, but on the opposite side. Even now, Orion and Scorpius can never be seen in the sky at the same time; when one rises, the other sets.

The Pleiades: The Seven Sisters

The Pleiades is a small but beautiful cluster of stars, often known as the "Seven Sisters." In Greek mythology, the Pleiades were seven sisters, the daughters of the titan Atlas and the sea nymph Pleione. Each of the sisters had their own story, but they were all admired for their beauty. According to legend, Orion the Hunter fell in love with the sisters and pursued them across the sky. To protect them, Zeus transformed the sisters into stars.

The Pleiades star cluster is visible in many parts of the world, and different cultures have their own stories about it. In Japan, the Pleiades are called Subaru, which means "unite." This name was later used for the famous car brand, and if you look at the Subaru logo, you'll see a pattern of stars based on the Pleiades cluster. Many Native American tribes, like the Navajo and

Cherokee, also have stories about the Pleiades, seeing them as a symbol of family, unity, and protection.

Draco: The Dragon in the Sky

In the northern sky, winding between the Big and Little Bears, you'll find Draco, the dragon. Draco is one of the oldest constellations, and it's been a part of stories from many ancient cultures. The Greeks imagined Draco as Ladon, a dragon that guarded the golden apples in the garden of the Hesperides. According to the myth, Hercules was given the task of stealing these golden apples as one of his twelve labors. He eventually defeated Ladon and took the apples, but to honor the dragon's service, the gods placed Ladon in the sky as Draco.

Other cultures also saw dragons or serpent-like creatures in this group of stars. In ancient China, dragons were powerful symbols, and they were associated with strength, luck, and the emperor. The stars in Draco were part of the Chinese celestial dragon, which stretched across the sky, bringing rain and prosperity to the land. To the Norse people of Scandinavia, Draco represented the dragon Nidhogg, a creature from their mythology that gnawed at the roots of the World Tree, Yggdrasil.

Scorpius: The Stinger of Orion

Scorpius, the Scorpion, has a tail that curls and a shape that's easy to recognize, especially in the summer sky. As you might remember from Orion's story, Scorpius was the giant scorpion sent by Gaia to stop the boastful hunter. After their legendary battle, both Orion and Scorpius were placed in the sky, but on opposite sides. That's why you'll never see Orion and Scorpius in the sky at the same time—they chase each other across the heavens, but they never meet.

In Polynesian mythology, Scorpius has a different story. The constellation's curve represents the fishhook of the demigod Maui. According to legend, Maui used his magical fishhook to pull up islands from the ocean, creating the Hawaiian Islands. In this part of the world, Scorpius is known as the Fishhook of Maui, a reminder of how cultures around the globe see the same stars in different ways.

Taurus: The Bull of the Sky

Taurus, the bull, is a large constellation near Orion. It's easy to spot because it contains a bright star named Aldebaran, which forms the bull's eye, and the V-shaped group of stars that represent the bull's face. According to Greek mythology, Taurus represents Zeus in disguise. The story goes that Zeus, king of the gods, transformed himself into a white bull to win the heart of Europa, a beautiful princess. Europa was so enchanted by the gentle bull that she climbed onto its back, and Zeus carried her across the sea to the island of Crete. To remember this event, Zeus placed the image of the bull in the night sky as Taurus.

In ancient Egypt, Taurus was associated with fertility and rebirth. The Egyptians saw the bull as a symbol of strength and life, and they celebrated it in their art and religion. In some Native American cultures, Taurus represents a bison, an animal important for survival, strength, and community.

Leo: The King of the Beasts

Leo, the lion, is a proud and powerful constellation. In Greek mythology, Leo represents the Nemean Lion, a creature that had a hide so tough it was nearly impossible to pierce. This lion was one of the challenges Hercules faced in his twelve labors. Hercules eventually defeated the Nemean Lion by using his strength and wits, and the gods placed the lion in the sky to celebrate its courage and power.

Leo has been recognized as a lion in other cultures, too. In ancient Mesopotamia, the lion symbolized royalty and strength. The Egyptians also saw this group of stars as a lion, connecting it to their own beliefs about the sun and the power of the pharaoh.

The Milky Way and Beyond

The Milky Way is the galaxy we call home, and it's huge. In fact, it's so big that it would take light, which travels incredibly fast, about 100,000 years to go from one side of the Milky Way to the other. And remember, light travels at around 186,000 miles per second! The Milky Way contains about 100 billion stars, and our Sun is just one of them. If you think of the Milky Way as a giant city, then our solar system would be a tiny neighborhood within it. And if our solar system is a neighborhood, Earth is just one house on one of its streets.

The Milky Way has a shape that scientists call a spiral galaxy. If you could look at it from above, you'd see a bright center with long, swirling arms reaching out from it, like a pinwheel or a whirlpool. These arms are filled with stars, gas, and dust, where new stars are constantly being born. Our solar system is located in one of these arms, called the Orion Arm. We're about two-thirds of the way out from the center of the galaxy, which is a good place to be. The center of the Milky Way is a busy, crowded region with stars packed together closely, while the outer areas are quieter and more stable, making it safer for planets like ours.

At the center of the Milky Way lies something incredibly powerful: a supermassive black hole. This black hole, named Sagittarius A*, is millions of times more massive than our Sun, but it's packed into a small, dense area. Black holes have such strong gravity that not even light can escape them, which is why they appear dark. Stars, gas, and dust all orbit around this black hole, and while it doesn't "suck" things in like a vacuum cleaner, anything that gets too close will be pulled in by its intense gravitational force. Scientists are still studying this black hole, trying to understand more about how it formed and how it affects the rest of our galaxy.

Our galaxy, though vast and complex, is just one of billions. Beyond the Milky Way, there are galaxies of all shapes and sizes. Some are spiral galaxies like ours, with graceful arms that curve out from the center. Others are elliptical galaxies, which look more like smooth, egg-shaped clouds of stars. And then there are irregular galaxies, which don't have a defined shape at all; they look more like blobs of stars scattered unevenly. Each galaxy is unique, shaped by the forces of gravity, star formation, and sometimes even collisions with other galaxies.

One of our closest galactic neighbors is the Andromeda Galaxy, which is also a spiral galaxy. Andromeda is even larger than the Milky Way, containing around a trillion stars. Right now, it's about 2.5 million light-years away from us, which is still incredibly far, but in cosmic terms, Andromeda is relatively close. In fact, Andromeda and the Milky Way are on a slow-motion collision course. In about 4.5 billion years, the two galaxies are expected to merge. When they do, they'll create a new, larger galaxy, and the night sky will look very different from what we see today.

Galaxies don't just float around on their own; they often gather in groups or clusters. The Milky Way is part of a small group of galaxies called the Local Group, which includes about 50 galaxies, including Andromeda and a few smaller ones like the Triangulum Galaxy. Groups like ours can then become part of even larger structures called clusters, which can contain hundreds or even thousands of galaxies bound together by gravity. These clusters, in turn, are part of superclusters, the largest structures in the universe. The Local Group is part of a supercluster called the Laniakea Supercluster, a massive structure that stretches for hundreds of millions of light-years.

Galaxies aren't just beautiful and massive; they also help us understand how the universe began. Scientists believe that everything in the universe started with a huge explosion called the Big Bang, about 13.8 billion years ago. After the Big Bang, the universe began to expand, and it's been expanding ever since. Galaxies formed as gravity pulled together clumps of gas and dust, creating stars and planets. By studying galaxies of different ages, scientists can look back in time and learn more about how the universe has changed. Some of the light we see from distant galaxies started its journey billions of years ago, allowing us to see what those galaxies looked like in the past.

Within galaxies, stars go through their life cycles, from birth in vast clouds of gas to death in spectacular supernovas. When massive stars explode, they release heavy elements into space, which later become part of new stars and planets. This cycle of birth, life, and death has been going on in galaxies for billions of years, constantly creating new stars and worlds. Every element on Earth, from the iron in our blood to the calcium in our bones, was forged in the heart of a star and scattered by a supernova. In a way, galaxies are like factories that create the elements needed for life.

One of the most mind-blowing discoveries about galaxies came in the 1920s, when astronomer Edwin Hubble realized that galaxies are moving away from each other. This observation led to the discovery that the universe is expanding. Imagine blowing up a balloon and drawing dots on it. As the balloon expands, the dots move away from each other. This is similar to what's happening in the universe, only on a much larger scale. Hubble's discovery changed the way we understand space and led to the idea of the Big Bang.

Today, astronomers use powerful telescopes, like the Hubble Space Telescope, to study galaxies in incredible detail. These telescopes can see galaxies that are billions of light-years away, revealing galaxies as they were in the early universe. In the future, even more advanced telescopes like the James Webb Space Telescope will help scientists explore galaxies in even more detail, uncovering new mysteries about how stars and planets form and how galaxies evolve.

When we look up at the Milky Way or see pictures of galaxies far away, we're reminded of the vastness of space. Each galaxy is filled with billions of stars, and many of those stars may have planets orbiting them. Some of those planets could even be similar to Earth, with the potential for life. With billions of galaxies in the observable universe, the possibilities for what might be out there are endless.

4
TOOLS OF THE ASTRONOMER

Telescopes

The most common type of telescope people are familiar with is the optical telescope. These are the kinds that let us see visible light, the same kind of light our eyes can see. There are two main types of optical telescopes: refracting telescopes and reflecting telescopes.

Refracting Telescopes: The First Type of Telescope

Refracting telescopes, or "refractors," were the first type of telescope ever made. They use lenses to bend, or "refract," light to bring it into focus. You can think of a refracting telescope as a kind of giant magnifying glass. Light from a distant object, like a star or planet, enters the telescope through a big lens at the front, called the objective lens. This lens bends the light, focusing it into a point. An eyepiece lens then magnifies this point, allowing you to see the object up close.

The first refracting telescopes were created in the early 1600s, and one of the most famous early users was Galileo Galilei. Galileo didn't invent the telescope, but he improved it significantly and used it to study the heavens. With his telescope, Galileo saw mountains on the Moon, discovered four of Jupiter's moons, and even noticed that Venus went through phases like the Moon. His discoveries changed the way people understood the universe.

Refracting telescopes are known for giving sharp, clear images, which is why they're popular for viewing planets and the Moon. However, they do have some downsides. Large lenses can be heavy and hard to make, and they can create a slight rainbow effect around objects, called chromatic aberration. Chromatic aberration happens because lenses bend different colors of light by different amounts, which can make the edges of objects look blurry or colorful. Despite this, refracting telescopes are still widely used, especially in smaller telescopes meant for beginners.

Reflecting Telescopes: Using Mirrors Instead of Lenses

While refracting telescopes use lenses, reflecting telescopes use mirrors to gather and focus light. This design was developed by Sir Isaac Newton in the late 1600s. Newton realized that mirrors could be used to create a clearer image without the chromatic aberration problem that lenses have. In a reflecting telescope, light enters the telescope and hits a large curved mirror at the back, called the primary mirror. This mirror reflects the light to a focal point, where a smaller mirror or eyepiece directs the light to your eye.

Reflecting telescopes, or "reflectors," are very popular among astronomers today, partly because mirrors are easier and cheaper to make than large lenses. Unlike lenses, mirrors don't have to be made from special materials to avoid chromatic aberration. Reflectors also allow for larger telescopes because you can make bigger mirrors without adding too much weight.

The largest telescopes in the world are all reflectors. These include massive observatories like the Keck Observatory in Hawaii, which uses two telescopes with mirrors that are 10 meters (about 33 feet) across. These huge mirrors can gather enormous amounts of light, allowing scientists to see very faint objects in space, like distant galaxies or faint nebulae.

Compound Telescopes: The Best of Both Worlds

While refracting and reflecting telescopes each have their strengths, there's also a third type of telescope called a compound telescope, or catadioptric telescope. Compound telescopes use both lenses and mirrors to gather and focus light, combining the advantages of both refractors and reflectors.

One popular type of compound telescope is the

Schmidt-Cassegrain telescope. In this design, light enters through a corrector lens, which helps fix some of the common issues with reflection, and then hits a primary mirror at the back of the telescope. The light is then reflected to a secondary mirror, which directs it through a hole in the primary mirror to the eyepiece.

Compound telescopes are versatile and compact, making them popular with amateur astronomers. They provide clear images, work well for both planets and deep-sky objects like galaxies, and are often easier to transport than large refractors or reflectors. However, they can be more expensive because they use both lenses and mirrors, which requires careful construction to get the best image quality.

Radio Telescopes: Listening to the Universe

Not all telescopes are used to look at visible light. Some telescopes are designed to "see" other types of energy, like radio waves. Radio telescopes are huge dish-shaped antennas that pick up radio waves from space. Unlike visible light, which can be blocked by clouds or the Earth's atmosphere, radio waves can travel through clouds, dust, and gas. This makes radio telescopes very useful for studying things we can't see with optical telescopes, like distant galaxies and cosmic events hidden behind gas clouds.

One of the most famous radio telescopes is the Arecibo Observatory in Puerto Rico, which was used to study everything from distant galaxies to asteroids and even to search for signals from intelligent life. Radio telescopes have shown us that the universe is full of things that don't give off visible light, like pulsars (rapidly spinning neutron stars) and quasars (extremely bright centers of distant galaxies). They help astronomers "listen" to space and uncover hidden secrets that optical telescopes can't reveal.

Space Telescopes: Observing Above the Atmosphere

Telescopes on Earth have one big challenge to deal with: the atmosphere. Earth's atmosphere is great for protecting us from harmful space radiation, but it also distorts and absorbs light, making it harder to get clear images. This is why scientists started sending telescopes into space, where there's no atmosphere to get in the way.

The Hubble Space Telescope, launched in 1990, was one of the first and most famous space telescopes. Floating high above Earth's atmosphere, Hubble has taken some of the most detailed pictures of space ever captured. It has shown us the beauty of distant galaxies, star clusters, and nebulae, and has helped scientists measure the expansion of the universe. Hubble has been working for over 30 years and continues to send back stunning images and valuable data.

Space telescopes aren't limited to visible light, either. The James Webb Space Telescope, set to be the successor to Hubble, will look at infrared light, which is useful for studying objects hidden by dust clouds. Infrared light can pass through dust more easily than visible light, allowing astronomers to study things like newly formed stars or the faint heat signals of distant galaxies.

Telescopes for Different Wavelengths: Seeing the Invisible Universe

The universe emits light and energy in a range of wavelengths beyond what our eyes can see. Along with radio and infrared telescopes, there are also telescopes for ultraviolet, X-ray, and gamma-ray wavelengths. These types of telescopes reveal parts of the universe that are invisible to the human eye.

Ultraviolet telescopes help scientists study hot, young stars and the regions around them. X-ray telescopes, like the Chandra X-ray Observatory, reveal high-energy events, such as black holes consuming material and neutron stars spinning rapidly. Gamma-ray telescopes capture the highest-energy events in the universe, like gamma-ray bursts from supernovae or merging neutron stars. Each type of telescope adds a piece to the puzzle of understanding the universe.

How Telescopes Have Changed Astronomy

Telescopes have come a long way from the simple refractors used by Galileo. Today, astronomers use powerful, specialized telescopes to study everything from nearby planets to the edges of the universe. Telescopes allow us to look back in time, as light from distant objects takes millions or even billions of years to reach us. They help us explore how stars are born, how galaxies evolve, and even what the universe looked like in its earliest moments.

Other Tools: Satellites, space probes, and observatories.

Satellites: Eyes in the Sky

A satellite is an object that orbits around a larger object, like a planet or star. Some satellites are natural, like the Moon orbiting Earth. But most of the satellites we think of in space are artificial—machines launched from Earth to orbit and collect data. Some satellites are designed to look back at Earth, helping us understand our weather, climate, and even to guide our GPS systems. Other satellites are built to look out into space, studying stars, planets, and galaxies from above the interference of Earth's atmosphere.

The Hubble Space Telescope is actually a type of satellite, one that orbits Earth and takes pictures of deep space. But Hubble is just one example. Satellites come in many forms and serve all sorts of purposes. For instance, the Chandra X-ray Observatory is a satellite that orbits Earth to observe X-rays coming from high-energy places in the universe, like black holes and exploding stars. Satellites like Chandra are essential because Earth's atmosphere blocks X-rays from reaching the ground, so we need to observe them from space.

Earth-observing satellites, like those from NASA's Earth Observing System, watch over our planet day and night, tracking changes in the climate, mapping forests, monitoring volcanic activity, and measuring sea levels. They're like guardians, constantly gathering information that helps scientists understand Earth's changing environment.

Space Probes: Journeys to the Unknown

While satellites usually stay in orbit around Earth or another planet, space probes are built to travel much farther. Probes are robotic explorers that leave Earth and journey through the solar system, carrying instruments to gather information about distant planets, moons, asteroids, and comets. They're incredibly important because they go where humans can't (yet) go. Once they reach their destination, space probes send back images and data that help scientists learn about worlds we can only imagine.

One of the most famous space probes is Voyager 1. Launched in 1977, Voyager 1 was designed to explore the outer planets. It flew by Jupiter and Saturn, taking close-up pictures and gathering data that no one had ever seen before. Today, Voyager 1 is the farthest human-made object from Earth, traveling beyond our solar system into interstellar space. Even now, over 40 years after it was launched, it continues to send back information about the outer reaches of the solar system, giving us a glimpse of what lies beyond the Sun's influence.

Another well-known space probe is New Horizons, which was launched in 2006 and traveled to Pluto. For years, Pluto was just a tiny dot in our telescopes, but when New Horizons finally reached it in 2015, it sent back incredible images and data that changed our understanding of this distant dwarf planet. We discovered mountains of ice, a heart-shaped glacier, and evidence of an atmosphere. New Horizons has continued past Pluto, heading deeper into the Kuiper Belt, a region filled with icy objects and other dwarf planets.

Mars has been visited by many probes, including the Viking landers, which were the first to touch down on the Martian surface in the 1970s. Since then, Mars has hosted an entire fleet of robotic explorers, from the Curiosity rover to the Perseverance rover, which is currently exploring the surface and even preparing samples to one day return to Earth. Each Mars probe has helped us understand the Red Planet better, revealing details about its dry riverbeds, ancient lakes, and the possibility that it once supported life.

Observatories: Collecting Data from Around the World

Observatories are special facilities designed for observing and studying celestial objects, like stars, planets, and galaxies. Some observatories are on mountaintops, where the air is thinner and clearer, reducing the interference from Earth's atmosphere. These observatories house some of the most powerful telescopes in the world, allowing scientists to capture incredibly detailed images and measurements of the universe.

One famous observatory is the Mauna Kea Observatories in Hawaii. Sitting high atop a dormant volcano, Mauna Kea offers some of the clearest views of the sky on Earth. Observatories here are equipped with massive telescopes that can study everything from nearby planets to distant galaxies. Observatories like these are also used to detect new phenomena, like black holes and exoplanets (planets orbiting other stars).

Another well-known observatory is the Arecibo Observatory, which was located in Puerto Rico until its collapse in 2020. Arecibo was a radio observatory, meaning it was designed to pick up radio waves from space. Its giant dish, which spanned 1,000 feet, helped astronomers study things that give off radio waves, like pulsars, quasars, and even distant galaxies. Arecibo was also used to send and listen for signals in the search for extraterrestrial intelligence (SETI).

Some observatories specialize in detecting other types of signals from space. For example, LIGO (Laser Interferometer Gravitational-Wave Observatory) is designed to detect gravitational waves, which are ripples in space-time caused by massive events, like the collision of black holes. When LIGO detected gravitational waves for the first time in 2015, it confirmed a prediction made by Albert Einstein a century earlier. This discovery opened up a new way of "seeing" the universe, allowing us to study events that don't produce light or radio waves.

The International Space Station: A Laboratory in Space

The International Space Station (ISS) is another unique tool for astronomy, but it's also much more. The ISS is a massive space station orbiting Earth, where astronauts live and work for months at a time. Scientists use the ISS as a laboratory to study how things work in space, without the effects of Earth's gravity. It's like a floating science lab, where experiments on everything from plants to physics help scientists understand how life and materials behave in space.

Astronomers on the ISS can also observe space without the interference of Earth's atmosphere. Astronauts often take stunning photographs of Earth, the Moon, and other celestial bodies from the ISS. And because it orbits Earth quickly, circling the planet about once every 90 minutes, the ISS gets different views of space throughout the day, making it an ideal spot for certain kinds of observations.

In addition to helping with astronomy, the ISS is preparing us for future exploration. Experiments conducted on the ISS help scientists understand how long-term space travel affects the human body, a key area of study for planning missions to Mars and beyond.

The Future of Space Exploration: New Tools and Missions

As technology advances, the tools for exploring space continue to improve. New telescopes like the James Webb Space Telescope will help scientists look deeper into space than ever before, studying the formation of galaxies, stars, and even planets. James Webb will look at the universe in infrared light, which is perfect for studying objects hidden by dust clouds, like newly forming stars and distant galaxies.

Another exciting area of exploration is the development of new probes and landers to explore moons and planets that we've only begun to study. Missions to Europa, one of Jupiter's moons, and Titan, one of Saturn's moons, are in the planning stages. Both of these moons are thought to have oceans beneath their icy crusts, raising the possibility of life.

How to Stargaze: Tips for beginner astronomers.

Stargazing is one of the simplest and most rewarding ways to explore space, and the best part is that you don't need any fancy equipment to get started. Just by stepping outside on a clear night and looking up, you can discover patterns in the stars, spot planets, and learn about the wonders of the universe. It's an activity that humans have been enjoying for thousands of years, and every night offers something a little different to see.

If you're interested in learning how to stargaze like an astronomer, there are some tips and tricks to make your experience even better. With a little patience, curiosity, and a few basic tools, you can start spotting planets, constellations, and maybe even a meteor or two.

Find a Dark Spot

The first step to good stargazing is to find a place with as little light as possible. Light pollution from streetlights, buildings, and cars can make it hard to see stars, especially the fainter ones. If you live in a city or a well-lit area, try finding a park, a field, or any open space away from the lights. Even if you don't live in the middle of nowhere, just moving away from bright lights can make a huge difference.

On especially dark nights, you might even see the Milky Way, our galaxy, stretching across the sky as a faint band of light. It's one of the most amazing sights in the night sky, and it's something that light pollution can easily hide. The darker your location, the more stars and celestial objects you'll be able to see, so it's worth finding a good stargazing spot.

Let Your Eyes Adjust

When you first step outside at night, everything may look dark and dim. This is because your eyes need time to adjust to the darkness. It takes about 20-30 minutes for your eyes to fully adapt to low light.

During this time, your pupils widen to let in as much light as possible, and special cells in your eyes called rods become more active, helping you see better in the dark.

While your eyes are adjusting, avoid looking at any bright lights, including your phone screen, as this can undo your progress and make it harder to see faint stars. If you need a light to check a star chart or map, try using a flashlight with a red filter or covering a regular flashlight with red cellophane. Red light is less harsh on your eyes and won't affect your night vision as much.

Start with the Big and Bright Stars

When you're new to stargazing, it can be overwhelming to look up and see so many stars scattered across the sky. A good way to start is by focusing on the brightest stars, which are easier to spot and can act as guides to help you find constellations. Some of the brightest stars include Sirius, Vega, and Arcturus, each of which has its own story and place in the sky.

Sirius, for example, is the brightest star in the night sky and is part of the constellation Canis Major, or the Great Dog. Once you spot Sirius, you can use it to help find other stars and constellations nearby. Arcturus is another bright star that's part of the constellation Boötes, and it's easy to spot during spring and summer in the northern hemisphere.

Learning to recognize a few bright stars can help you get your bearings and make finding constellations much easier. Think of them as stepping stones that guide you around the night sky.

Learn the Constellations

Constellations are groups of stars that form patterns, like pictures in the sky. Learning the constellations can make stargazing even more fun, as each one has its own name, story, and history. You don't need to learn them all at once; start with a few that are easy to find, like the Big Dipper, Orion, and Scorpius.

The Big Dipper is a great place to begin because it's visible year-round in the northern hemisphere and has a shape that's easy to recognize. It looks like a ladle or a scoop, and it's part of a larger constellation called Ursa Major, or the Great Bear. Once you can spot the Big Dipper, you can use it to find other constellations. For example, the two stars at the end of the Big Dipper's "bowl" point toward Polaris, the North Star.

Orion, the Hunter, is another easily recognizable constellation, especially during winter. Orion has a distinct "belt" of three stars in a row, which makes it stand out from other constellations. Knowing where to find Orion's belt can help you locate nearby constellations, like Taurus and Canis Major.

As you learn more constellations, you'll start to see how they fit together like a map. Many stargazers use star charts or apps to help them identify constellations. Star charts are like maps of the sky, showing the position of stars and constellations for different times of the year. Apps can be especially handy because they often have features that show you the sky in real time, based on your location.

Look for Planets

Planets are some of the most exciting things to see in the night sky. Unlike stars, which twinkle, planets usually appear as steady, bright points of light. The brightest planets are Venus, Jupiter, Mars, and Saturn, and they're often visible with the naked eye. Because they orbit the Sun like Earth, they move across the sky from night to night, which makes finding them a fun challenge.

Venus is usually the easiest planet to spot because it's incredibly bright. It's often called the "Evening Star" or "Morning Star" because it shines brightly near the horizon just after sunset or before sunrise. Jupiter and Saturn are also quite bright and can often be seen in the southern sky, depending on the season. Mars has a reddish color that makes it stand out from stars, especially when it's close to Earth.

Using a planet chart or app can help you figure out which planets are visible in the sky on a given night. Once you spot a planet, it's exciting to watch its position change over days and weeks as it moves in its orbit.

Watch for Meteor Showers

Meteor showers are another amazing sight in the night sky. They happen when Earth passes through a trail of debris left behind by a comet. When these small bits of rock and dust enter Earth's atmosphere, they burn up, creating bright streaks of light called meteors, or "shooting stars."

Some of the most famous meteor showers include the Perseids in August, the Geminids in December, and the Quadrantids in January. Each meteor shower is named after the constellation where the meteors appear to originate, so during the Perseids, the meteors seem to come from the constellation Perseus.

You don't need any special equipment to watch a meteor shower. Just find a dark spot, lie back, and watch the sky. Meteor showers are best seen after midnight when Earth is facing into the trail of debris. If you're lucky, you might see dozens of meteors in a single night!

Use Binoculars for a Closer Look

While you don't need a telescope to enjoy stargazing, binoculars can give you a closer view of the night sky. Binoculars are a great tool for beginner astronomers because they're easier to use than a telescope and can help you see details like the craters on the Moon, star clusters, and even some of Jupiter's moons.

Binoculars with a magnification of 7x or 10x work well for stargazing. They can help you see more stars in a constellation, explore the Milky Way, and spot details that aren't visible to the naked eye. Try pointing them at the Pleiades star cluster, a small group of stars that looks beautiful through binoculars.

Be Patient and Enjoy the Night Sky

One of the most important things to remember when stargazing is to be patient. The sky is vast, and there's a lot to see, but some things take time. Let yourself get comfortable, take a few deep breaths, and enjoy the peace of the night. You might not see everything at once, but each time you look, you'll discover something new.

5

EXPLORING SPACE
THE APOLLO MISSIONS: WALKING ON THE MOON

One of the most famous space missions in history was Apollo 11, the mission that first landed humans on the Moon. In the 1960s, there was a "space race" between the United States and the Soviet Union to see who could reach space first. Both countries wanted to prove they had the best technology and the bravest astronauts. The Soviet Union made the first big move in 1961 when cosmonaut Yuri Gagarin became the first human in space. Not long after, the United States set a goal that was even more ambitious: sending people to the Moon.

The Apollo program was created by NASA with the goal of putting a human on the Moon and bringing them back safely. After years of preparation and many test missions, NASA launched Apollo 11 on July 16, 1969. The spacecraft carried three astronauts: Neil

Armstrong, Buzz Aldrin, and Michael Collins. After traveling 240,000 miles from Earth, Apollo 11 reached the Moon, and on July 20, 1969, Neil Armstrong took that famous first step onto the lunar surface, saying, "That's one small step for man, one giant leap for mankind." Buzz Aldrin joined him, and together they spent a couple of hours exploring, collecting rock samples, and setting up experiments.

Michael Collins didn't walk on the Moon. He stayed in orbit around it, piloting the command module, which would take them all home. The Apollo 11 mission was a huge success and inspired millions of people around the world. In total, there were six Apollo missions that landed on the Moon, from Apollo 11 to Apollo 17. These missions taught us a lot about the Moon's surface, its rocks, and what it might be like to live and work there someday.

The Mars Rovers: Exploring the Red Planet

After the Moon, Mars became the next big focus for space exploration. Mars is sometimes called Earth's "sister planet" because it has seasons, polar ice caps, and a day that's only a little longer than ours. But Mars is also very different: it's a cold desert world with thin air and dust storms that can cover the entire planet. Scientists believe that Mars may have had liquid water on its surface billions of years ago, which raises the exciting possibility that it could have once supported life.

Since the 1970s, various missions have been sent to explore Mars, and some of the most famous are the Mars rovers. Rovers are robotic vehicles designed to drive across the Martian surface, taking photos, gathering samples, and conducting experiments. One of the first successful rovers was Sojourner, part of NASA's Pathfinder mission in 1997. Although Sojourner was only about the size of a microwave oven, it proved that a robotic vehicle could survive and move around on Mars.

In 2004, two more rovers, Spirit and Opportunity, were sent to Mars. These twin rovers were expected to last about three months, but they far exceeded that! Spirit continued to explore until 2010, and Opportunity amazed everyone by working for nearly 15 years, finally going silent in 2018 after a massive dust storm. During their missions, Spirit and Opportunity made many discoveries, including evidence of water in Mars's past, which added to the hope that life could have once existed there.

Curiosity, a much larger and more advanced rover, landed on Mars in 2012. Unlike the previous rovers, which relied on solar panels for power, Curiosity has a nuclear battery that lets it work through long winters and dust storms. Curiosity has explored Mars's Gale Crater, a site that scientists believe was once filled with water. It has found rocks and soil that contain ingredients necessary for life, like carbon, hydrogen, and oxygen. This discovery suggests that Mars may have been a more Earth-like planet billions of years ago.

The newest Mars rover, Perseverance, landed on Mars in 2021. Perseverance is exploring an ancient river delta in Jezero Crater, an area that scientists think could have been a habitat for life long ago. Perseverance is also collecting samples of Mars's soil and rocks to be returned to Earth by a future mission. It even brought along a tiny helicopter named Ingenuity, which made the first powered flights on another planet. Perseverance and Ingenuity are helping scientists prepare for the day when humans might finally walk on Mars.

Voyager: Traveling Beyond the Solar System

Another groundbreaking space mission is the Voyager program. In 1977, NASA launched two spacecraft, Voyager 1 and Voyager 2, to explore the outer planets of our solar system. Their mission was to study Jupiter, Saturn, Uranus, and Neptune, capturing images and data as they flew by each planet. The Voyagers sent back incredible pictures of these distant worlds, showing details like Jupiter's Great Red Spot (a massive storm) and Saturn's icy rings. Voyager 2 is still the only spacecraft to have visited Uranus and Neptune, revealing the mysterious bluish color of their atmospheres.

After their main mission was complete, the Voyagers kept going. Voyager 1 is now the farthest human-made object from Earth, traveling in interstellar space—the region between stars. Both Voyagers carry a "Golden Record," a special message intended for any intelligent life that might find them. The record contains sounds of Earth, including music, greetings in multiple languages, and even the sound of a heartbeat. These records are like a cosmic greeting card, introducing Earth to the universe.

Cassini-Huygens: Discovering Saturn and Its Moons

One of the most exciting missions to the outer solar system was the Cassini-Huygens mission to Saturn, launched in 1997. Cassini reached Saturn in 2004 and spent 13 years orbiting the planet, taking stunning photos and gathering information about Saturn's rings, atmosphere, and moons. Cassini gave us our first detailed look at Saturn's rings, showing that they're made of countless particles of ice and rock.

Cassini also explored Saturn's moons, including Enceladus and Titan. Enceladus was one of the most surprising discoveries. Cassini found that this small, icy moon has geysers that shoot water vapor and ice particles into space, suggesting there's a liquid ocean beneath its frozen surface. Scientists think Enceladus could potentially support life in its underground ocean.

Titan, Saturn's largest moon, is another fascinating world. Cassini released a probe called Huygens, which parachuted down to Titan's surface, making it the first landing on a moon other than our own. Titan has lakes and rivers—not of water, but of liquid methane and ethane, which flow and evaporate in a cycle similar to water on Earth. Titan's thick atmosphere and organic compounds make it an intriguing place to study, as it could hold clues about how life began on Earth.

The International Space Station: Living and Working in Space

While the Apollo missions and Mars rovers have focused on exploring specific places, the International Space Station (ISS) is a mission that allows people to live and work in space. The ISS orbits Earth about every 90 minutes, giving astronauts a unique view of our planet and the opportunity to conduct science experiments in microgravity.

Since its launch in 1998, the ISS has hosted astronauts from around the world. It serves as a laboratory for studying how space affects the human body, plants, and even materials. Experiments on the ISS are helping scientists learn more about how to live and work in space for long periods, which is important for future missions to Mars or beyond. Astronauts on the ISS also help maintain and upgrade the station, making it a continuously evolving mission in space.

Life of an Astronaut: Training, space travel, and daily life in space.

Training to Become an Astronaut

The road to becoming an astronaut starts with

some serious training. Astronauts need to learn a wide range of skills because space travel is unpredictable, and there's no calling a repairman or doctor if something goes wrong. They train for years to be ready for anything, from handling emergencies to doing scientific experiments.

Astronaut candidates usually have a background in science, engineering, or aviation. Some are pilots, while others are scientists or doctors. They all have to be in excellent physical shape because space travel is hard on the body. Once selected, candidates begin training at places like NASA's Johnson Space Center in Houston, Texas.

One of the first things they learn is how to handle weightlessness, or microgravity, the feeling of floating that astronauts experience in space. To practice, astronauts train on a special aircraft nicknamed the "Vomit Comet." This plane flies in large arcs, going up and then dropping quickly, creating short periods of weightlessness. During these moments, astronauts experience the feeling of floating just like they would in space. It's one of the best ways to prepare for the strange sensation of being weightless, though it can take some getting used to!

Astronauts also spend a lot of time in a giant swimming pool called the Neutral Buoyancy Lab. This pool is big enough to fit a full-size model of the International Space Station (ISS), and astronauts wear weighted suits to simulate microgravity underwater.

Working in the water allows them to practice spacewalks, learning how to move and handle tools while floating. They practice fixing equipment, attaching cables, and building structures, all while floating, which is harder than it sounds. Working in space is all about patience and precision because even the smallest movement can send you drifting.

On top of physical training, astronauts also go through intense classroom lessons. They need to learn how to operate spacecraft systems, navigate in space, conduct science experiments, and even speak multiple languages. The ISS is an international effort, so astronauts often learn Russian to communicate with their Russian colleagues. They also practice working as a team because cooperation is essential in space, where every astronaut depends on the others.

The Launch: Leaving Earth Behind

After years of training, astronauts are finally ready for the big day: launch. A launch day is filled with excitement, nerves, and last-minute preparations. Astronauts put on their spacesuits, which are specially designed to protect them in case of any problems during the launch. They check their equipment, say goodbye to their families, and then make their way to the spacecraft. It's a powerful moment, filled with both excitement and focus.

When the rocket engines ignite, astronauts are pushed back into their seats with incredible force as they leave Earth's gravity behind. They feel a pressure called "G-force," which is like an intense weight pressing down on them. For the first few minutes, they're moving at thousands of miles per hour as the rocket carries them through the atmosphere. Once the rocket reaches space, they feel the engines cut off, and suddenly, everything is quiet, and they begin to float. They've arrived in microgravity, and from this point forward, everything will feel weightless.

Daily Life in Space: Eating, Sleeping, and Working

Life in space is full of unusual challenges. Without gravity, even simple tasks like eating, sleeping, and brushing your teeth have to be done differently. Astronauts learn to adapt quickly, making the most of every moment and keeping things organized in their floating environment.

Eating in space is a fun but messy task. Food doesn't stay on a plate, so astronauts use specially packaged meals. Some foods are freeze-dried, which means they've had all the water removed and need to be rehydrated before eating. Astronauts add water to these packages and then eat directly from them with a spoon. Other foods are sealed in pouches or tubes to prevent crumbs, which would float around and could get stuck in equipment. Drinks are also in pouches with straws to prevent spills. There are some fun treats too—astronauts can even eat tortillas instead of bread because tortillas don't create crumbs!

Sleeping in space is also very different. There's no

"up" or "down" in microgravity, so astronauts can sleep in any direction. They have sleeping bags attached to the walls, which keep them from floating around while they rest. Inside their sleeping bags, they drift off to sleep, floating comfortably. Astronauts usually get about 8 hours of sleep, but sometimes, it's hard to sleep because the ISS orbits Earth every 90 minutes, meaning they see a sunrise or sunset 16 times a day! Special eye masks and earplugs help block out the changing light and noises on the station.

Working is the main focus for astronauts on the ISS, and every day is packed with tasks. They conduct science experiments to learn more about how plants grow in space, how bacteria behave, and how the human body changes without gravity. These experiments help scientists understand more about space and prepare for future missions, including long trips to Mars. Astronauts also perform maintenance on the ISS itself, keeping it running smoothly. They check air filters, repair equipment, and make sure everything is working correctly. They even exercise for about two hours a day because, in microgravity, muscles and bones can weaken without regular use.

One of the most exciting parts of an astronaut's job is the spacewalk. A spacewalk, or extravehicular activity (EVA), is when an astronaut leaves the safety of the space station to work outside in space. Dressed in a bulky spacesuit with oxygen, cooling systems, and a visor to block the Sun's glare, astronauts step outside and float in space. They might install new equipment, repair broken parts, or test tools for future missions. A spacewalk can last up to eight hours, and astronauts train extensively to be ready for this challenging task.

Staying Connected with Earth

Even though astronauts are far from home, they stay in touch with friends, family, and colleagues on Earth. The ISS has communication systems that allow astronauts to send emails, make video calls, and even talk to people live through radio. Sometimes, astronauts do interviews with schools or TV stations, sharing what life in space is like and inspiring the next generation of space explorers.

Astronauts also have a little bit of free time each day. They might read, listen to music, watch movies, or even look out the window. The ISS has a special viewing area called the Cupola, a dome with windows that gives astronauts a 360-degree view of Earth and space. From the Cupola, they can see continents, oceans, and even city lights. They often say that seeing Earth from space is one of the most awe-inspiring parts of the experience.

Returning to Earth: Reentry and Adjustment

After weeks or months in space, it's time for astronauts to return home. Reentry, or coming back through Earth's atmosphere, is another challenging part of the journey. The spacecraft must enter the atmosphere at just the right angle, or it could bounce off or burn up. As the spacecraft descends, astronauts feel the G-forces again, pressing them into their seats as they come closer to Earth's surface.

Once they land, astronauts have to adjust to gravity all over again. After floating for so long, even lifting an arm can feel heavy. They might feel wobbly or have trouble standing up straight, but after a few days, their bodies start to feel normal again. Returning to Earth is a reminder of how different life in space really is and how much the human body has to adapt.

The International Space Station: What it is and what happens there.

High above Earth, orbiting at about 250 miles above us, is an incredible scientific laboratory and home called the International Space Station, or ISS. The ISS is one of the most impressive creations of modern technology and teamwork. It's about the size of a football field and moves incredibly fast—zooming around Earth at 17,500 miles per hour. At this speed, the astronauts on board see a sunrise or sunset every 90 minutes!

The ISS isn't just a spacecraft; it's a place where astronauts live, work, and explore the unknowns of space. Built by a partnership of five space agencies—the United States' NASA, Russia's Roscosmos, Japan's JAXA, Europe's ESA, and Canada's CSA—the ISS has been home to astronauts from around the world since the year 2000. This "floating laboratory" is a place where people live in microgravity and study how the human body and other living things adapt to life without gravity.

Building the ISS: A Global Effort

The ISS was built piece by piece, like a giant puzzle in space. Since it was too large to launch all at once, different parts were launched separately and assembled in orbit. Each module, or section, was carried by rockets and space shuttles over many years, and astronauts connected them together like giant building blocks. The first module, called Zarya, was launched in 1998, and new modules have been added and upgraded over the years to make the ISS what it is today.

Building the ISS was a huge accomplishment in teamwork. Scientists, engineers, and astronauts from different countries worked together to design and assemble it. Each module has a specific purpose, like providing power, housing scientific labs, or creating living quarters for astronauts. The ISS is a true symbol of international cooperation, showing how people from different backgrounds can unite to achieve something extraordinary.

Life on the ISS: Floating Homes and Workspaces

Life on the ISS is unique and challenging, especially because there's no gravity. Astronauts float around as they move from one section to another. Living on the ISS means adapting to an environment where "up" and "down" don't really exist, and objects can float away if they're not secured.

Each astronaut has a small personal area to call

their own. They sleep in tiny compartments attached to the wall, using sleeping bags to keep them from floating around as they sleep. Astronauts have to get used to some unusual routines on the ISS. For example, brushing your teeth in microgravity requires a bit of creativity: you can't just spit out toothpaste, because it would float around. Instead, astronauts either swallow it or wipe it with a cloth. Showering isn't possible either; instead, they use wet wipes and rinse-free shampoo to stay clean.

Meals on the ISS come in special packages designed for space. Food needs to be carefully prepared so it doesn't create crumbs, which would float around and clog the equipment. Many foods are freeze-dried or packed in vacuum-sealed pouches. To eat, astronauts add water to rehydrate meals and use forks and spoons with Velcro on the handles to keep them from floating away. It's not fancy dining, but it's all part of the space adventure!

Science on the ISS: Experiments in Microgravity

The main purpose of the ISS is to be a scientific laboratory where astronauts can conduct experiments that aren't possible on Earth. The ISS has research labs from different countries, and these labs are packed with equipment to study biology, physics, chemistry, and even materials science. Since gravity affects everything on Earth, studying things in microgravity allows scientists to see how they behave in new ways.

One area of research focuses on understanding

how living in space affects the human body. Astronauts experience changes in their muscles, bones, and even their vision while in microgravity. Muscles can weaken, and bones lose density because they don't have to support the body's weight. By studying these changes, scientists learn about how to keep astronauts healthy for long-duration missions, like a future trip to Mars.

Plants are another focus on the ISS. Learning how plants grow in space could be essential for future space missions, as astronauts would need fresh food if they traveled far from Earth. On the ISS, scientists study how seeds sprout, roots grow, and plants adapt to life in microgravity. This research also helps us understand more about plant growth here on Earth and could lead to improvements in agriculture.

Another exciting area of research is fluid dynamics. Fluids behave differently without gravity, forming bubbles or floating in ways we don't see on Earth. This information is useful for designing better water systems, fuel tanks, and other technology for space and for Earth. There are even experiments on fire and combustion, which act differently in space than they do on Earth. By studying fire in microgravity, scientists can improve safety measures both on Earth and in space.

The ISS also serves as a platform for studying space itself. Instruments outside the station observe cosmic rays, solar radiation, and other space phenomena. The ISS offers scientists a unique vantage point to study Earth as well. From this high up, they can monitor weather patterns, study ocean currents, and observe environmental changes, helping scientists understand more about Earth's climate and atmosphere.

Exercise and Health: Staying Strong in Space

Living in microgravity might sound fun, but it presents challenges for staying healthy. Without gravity, muscles and bones don't get the same workout they do on Earth, and this can lead to serious weakening. To counter this, astronauts exercise for about two hours every day. The ISS has a treadmill, an exercise bike, and a resistance machine called ARED (Advanced Resistive Exercise Device) to help astronauts maintain their muscle and bone strength.

Working out in microgravity isn't quite the same as working out on Earth. Astronauts use harnesses to strap themselves to the treadmill and resistance bands for weightlifting exercises, allowing them to mimic the effects of gravity. These workouts are essential for astronauts' health, especially for when they return to Earth and have to readjust to full gravity.

Spacewalks: Working Outside the ISS

One of the most challenging and exciting tasks on the ISS is the spacewalk, also known as an EVA (extravehicular activity). Spacewalks are when astronauts leave the ISS to work outside in space. Spacewalks might involve installing new equipment, fixing broken parts, or running tests for future missions.

Before a spacewalk, astronauts put on a specially designed suit that provides oxygen, regulates temperature, and protects them from the harsh environment of space. The suits are bulky and heavy on Earth, but in space, the weight doesn't matter, though the size can still make it tricky to move. A spacewalk can last anywhere from four to eight hours, and astronauts must be careful with every movement, as one wrong move could send them drifting away.

Every spacewalk is carefully planned, with teams on Earth guiding astronauts step-by-step to complete the mission. Astronauts also practice spacewalks in the Neutral Buoyancy Lab (NBL), a massive swimming pool on Earth, which simulates the feeling of microgravity. Each spacewalk is a test of teamwork, precision, and skill, and every successful mission makes the ISS safer and more effective.

The Future of the ISS: A Gateway to Mars and Beyond

The ISS is not only a laboratory but also a stepping stone for future exploration. The knowledge and experience gained here help scientists and engineers design spacecraft, habitats, and technology that could one day take humans to Mars. Astronauts on the ISS learn about the challenges of long-term space living, such as radiation exposure, isolation, and limited resources.

There are plans for the ISS to eventually transition from a government-funded project to a privately funded one, with commercial companies possibly using it as a research base. NASA is also developing the Gateway, a small space station that will orbit the Moon. The Gateway will serve as a base for lunar missions and as a testing ground for the technology needed for Mars missions.

6

EXOPLANETS AND THE SEARCH FOR LIFE

The idea of exoplanets isn't entirely new. People have wondered about other worlds for centuries. Even in ancient times, some philosophers thought the stars could have planets orbiting them, just like our Sun has its family of planets. But it wasn't until the 1990s that scientists actually discovered the first exoplanet. Since then, with the help of powerful telescopes and clever techniques, we've found thousands of them. Exoplanets are now one of the most exciting fields in astronomy, and every year we learn more about them.

How We Find Exoplanets

You might think that finding exoplanets is as simple as pointing a telescope at a star and spotting a planet nearby, but it's not that easy. Exoplanets are incredibly far away, and they're often hidden by the bright light of the stars they orbit. Trying to see a small, dark planet near a bright star is like trying to spot a firefly next to a streetlamp. But scientists have developed some clever techniques to find exoplanets without directly seeing them.

One of the main methods is called the transit method. Imagine watching a tiny ant crawl across the face of a flashlight. As the ant moves across, it blocks a tiny bit of the light, causing a small dip in brightness. This is similar to what happens when an exoplanet crosses in front of its star from our point of view. Astronomers watch for these small dips in a star's brightness, which can happen each time the planet orbits in front of the star. By studying the pattern and size of these dips, scientists can learn about the planet's size, how close it is to its star, and even the length of its year.

Another method is the radial velocity technique, also known as the "wobble" method. Just like planets are pulled by the gravity of their stars, stars are also pulled a little bit by the planets that orbit them. This causes the star to "wobble" slightly as the planet moves around it. Astronomers can detect this wobble by studying the star's light, which shifts slightly in color as the star moves. By measuring the wobble, scientists can determine the planet's mass and its distance from the star.

Some exoplanets have even been found using

direct imaging, which is exactly what it sounds like—taking a picture of the planet itself. This is extremely challenging because the star's light usually overwhelms the planet's faint glow. However, with advanced techniques like blocking the starlight or using special filters, astronomers have managed to capture images of some exoplanets directly.

Different Types of Exoplanets

Exoplanets come in an amazing variety of sizes, compositions, and distances from their stars. Some are similar to the planets we find in our own solar system, like Earth-sized rocky planets or gas giants similar to Jupiter. But many exoplanets are unlike anything we've seen close to home.

One of the most common types of exoplanets discovered so far are gas giants called "Hot Jupiters." These planets are similar in size to Jupiter, but they orbit extremely close to their stars, making them incredibly hot. Because of their closeness to the star, Hot Jupiters have short years, sometimes lasting only a few days. Their temperatures can soar to thousands of degrees, making them hostile worlds with intense heat and turbulent atmospheres.

Then there are super-Earths, which are rocky planets like Earth but larger in size. Super-Earths could be twice, three times, or even more massive than our planet, and scientists are very curious about them. These planets may have thick atmospheres, active volcanoes, and maybe even oceans. Some super-Earths might even have the right conditions to support life, depending on their distance from their star.

Another interesting type of exoplanet is the "water world." Water worlds are thought to be covered in oceans, with surfaces entirely made of liquid water. These planets are unlike anything in our solar system. Imagine a world where there's no land at all, just endless oceans stretching out as far as the eye can see. Scientists believe that life could potentially exist in the oceans of these water worlds, making them exciting targets for future exploration.

One of the most mysterious types of exoplanets is the "rogue planet." Rogue planets don't orbit any star at all; they float through space on their own, likely kicked out of their original star systems by gravitational forces. Without a star to provide light and warmth, these planets are dark and cold. Still, scientists are curious about them and wonder what conditions might be like on a planet drifting alone through the galaxy.

The Habitable Zone: Where Life Might Be Possible

When scientists look for exoplanets that might support life, they often focus on a region around each star called the "habitable zone." This is the area where conditions might be just right for liquid water to exist on a planet's surface. If a planet is too close to its star, it would be too hot, and any water would evaporate. If it's too far away, it would be too cold, and water would freeze. But if it's in the habitable zone, sometimes called the "Goldilocks zone," there's a chance that water could exist as a liquid, which is essential for life as we know it.

Not every planet in the habitable zone has liquid water or the right conditions for life, but it's a good place to start the search. Earth, for example, is in the Sun's habitable zone, which is why we have oceans, rivers, and lakes. Scientists have already found some exoplanets that are in the habitable zones of their stars, and these planets are top targets for future study.

One of the most exciting discoveries is a system called TRAPPIST-1, which has seven Earth-sized planets orbiting a cool, dim star. Three of these planets are located in the star's habitable zone, raising the possibility that they could have liquid water. TRAPPIST-1 is only 40 light-years away, which is relatively close in cosmic terms. Scientists are eagerly studying this system, hoping it might reveal clues about the potential for life.

Could There Be Life on Exoplanets?

The question of whether life exists on other planets is one of the biggest mysteries in science. On Earth, life exists in all kinds of environments, from deep ocean vents to icy polar regions, which makes scientists wonder if life could adapt to other worlds too. Life might look very different on an exoplanet, depending on its conditions, such as temperature, atmosphere, and the types of chemicals available.

Finding signs of life on an exoplanet would be challenging. Scientists look for "biosignatures," which are signs that life might be present. On Earth, certain gases like oxygen and methane are produced by living things, so finding these gases on another planet could be a clue. Future telescopes, like the James Webb Space Telescope, are designed to analyze the atmospheres of exoplanets, searching for biosignatures that could suggest life.

However, scientists also keep an open mind about what life might be like elsewhere. Life on other planets might not need the same conditions as Earth. Some scientists speculate about "extremophiles," which are life forms that thrive in extreme conditions on Earth, like hot springs or salty lakes. These extremophiles could help us imagine the types of life that might survive on other worlds with harsh environments, such as a hot, rocky planet or a freezing water world.

The Future of Exoplanet Exploration

The search for exoplanets is just beginning, and with each discovery, our understanding of the universe expands. Scientists are developing new telescopes and missions to help us find and study these distant worlds. The upcoming missions could reveal even more about the atmospheres, climates, and compositions of exoplanets, bringing us closer to understanding what they're truly like.

One future mission, known as the James Webb Space Telescope, is designed to see in infrared light, which is especially useful for studying planets that are far from their stars or hidden behind dust clouds. There's also the PLATO mission, set to search for Earth-sized exoplanets in the habitable zones of their stars, and the TESS mission, which is already scanning the skies to find more exoplanets close to Earth.

How We Find Exoplanets

The Transit Method: Watching for Tiny Dips in Starlight

One of the most successful methods for finding exoplanets is called the transit method. Picture a planet orbiting its star, like Earth orbits the Sun. If this planet's orbit lines up just right from our point of view, it will occasionally pass directly in front of its star. When it does, it blocks a tiny portion of the star's light, causing the star to look slightly dimmer for a brief time. This is known as a "transit," and it's like watching a small shadow cross the face of a light.

To detect these tiny dips in brightness, astronomers use space telescopes like the Kepler Space Telescope, which was designed specifically for finding exoplanets using the transit method. Kepler watched thousands of stars for long periods, looking for these tiny dips. By studying the timing and depth of each dip, scientists could determine a planet's size and how far it orbits from its star. This method has helped scientists find thousands of exoplanets, including many Earth-sized ones.

One exciting thing about the transit method is that it not only reveals a planet's size but can also give clues about its atmosphere. When a planet passes in front of its star, a tiny bit of starlight passes through the planet's atmosphere (if it has one). By studying the colors of this light, scientists can figure out which gases are present in the atmosphere. This technique, known as "transit spectroscopy," has helped scientists detect atmospheres around several exoplanets, and some even have clouds, which brings us one step closer to finding habitable worlds.

The Radial Velocity Method: Detecting a Star's "Wobble"

Another powerful method for finding exoplanets is called the radial velocity method, or the "wobble" method. Just as a planet is pulled by the gravity of its star, the star is also tugged a little bit by the planet's gravity. This causes the star to "wobble" slightly as the planet orbits around it. Although the star doesn't move as much as the planet does, this wobble is enough to be detected by studying the star's light.

Here's how it works: when a star wobbles due to the pull of a planet, its light shifts slightly in color. When the star moves towards us, its light shifts towards the blue end of the spectrum, and when it moves away, its light shifts towards the red end. This effect is called the Doppler shift, and it's the same effect you hear when a siren passes by—a high-pitched sound when it's coming towards you and a lower pitch as it moves away. Astronomers use special instruments to measure these shifts in a star's light and determine the "wobble" caused by orbiting planets.

The radial velocity method can tell scientists a lot about a planet, including its mass and how close it is to its star. Larger planets like gas giants create bigger wobbles, making them easier to detect, while smaller planets like Earth are harder to find with this method. Still, the radial velocity method has been a major tool in finding some of the first exoplanets and continues to help astronomers discover planets that orbit nearby stars.

Direct Imaging: Taking Pictures of Distant Worlds

Direct imaging is exactly what it sounds like: actually taking a picture of a planet outside our solar system. This might seem like the most obvious way to find an exoplanet, but it's also one of the hardest methods. Planets are incredibly dim compared to their stars, which shine millions or even billions of times brighter. It's almost like trying to spot a faint light right next to a super bright spotlight. But with advances in technology, scientists have managed to take pictures of a few exoplanets directly.

To capture these faint planets, astronomers use special techniques to block out the star's light. One common tool is called a coronagraph, which blocks the light from the star, making it easier to see the faint glow of planets nearby. Another approach is to use a special "starshade," which is like an umbrella placed in front of a telescope to block out the star's light.

Direct imaging has been successful in capturing images of large planets orbiting far from their stars. These planets are often gas giants, similar to Jupiter, but even larger. While direct imaging hasn't found as many exoplanets as the transit or radial velocity methods, it allows astronomers to study planets in ways other methods can't, like observing their atmosphere and temperature.

Microlensing: Using Gravity to Find Hidden Planets

One of the most unusual methods for finding exoplanets is called gravitational microlensing. Imagine you're watching a distant star, and suddenly, another star moves in front of it, like a cosmic magnifying glass. The gravity of the closer star bends and focuses the light from the distant star, causing it to brighten temporarily. This effect is called microlensing, and it can also reveal planets orbiting around the closer star.

If the closer star has a planet, the planet's gravity can create a smaller, additional magnification in the light from the distant star. This is a rare event, but when it happens, it can reveal planets that would otherwise be impossible to detect. The microlensing method is particularly good at finding planets that are farther from their stars, similar to where Jupiter and Saturn are in our solar system. It has even been used to discover rogue planets—planets that don't orbit any star but instead float freely through space.

Microlensing events don't last long, and they're unpredictable, which makes them challenging to study. However, organizations like the Optical Gravitational Lensing Experiment (OGLE) constantly monitor stars to catch these rare events. While this method doesn't find as many exoplanets as other techniques, it adds to our knowledge of distant planets and helps complete the picture of how planets are distributed in our galaxy.

Astrometry: Measuring Tiny Shifts in Stars' Positions

Astrometry is one of the oldest methods for detecting planets, but it's also one of the most difficult. It involves measuring tiny changes in a star's position in the sky caused by the gravitational pull of an orbiting planet. As a planet orbits its star, it makes the star wobble slightly. While this wobble is often too small to see, high-precision measurements can detect it.

Astrometry works best for finding planets around nearby stars, and it's especially useful for detecting planets with wide orbits. Although this method has been used for centuries in astronomy, it requires extremely precise measurements, so it hasn't been as successful as other methods. However, new space telescopes with advanced technology may make astrometry more effective in the future.

One advantage of astrometry is that it can provide a lot of information about a planet's orbit and position relative to its star. With further advances in technology, astrometry could become a more widely used method for detecting exoplanets, adding to the toolkit scientists use to explore distant worlds.

The Future of Exoplanet Detection

As technology improves, scientists are developing even more advanced ways to find and study exoplanets. Future telescopes, like the James Webb Space Telescope and the European Space Agency's PLATO mission, are designed to be incredibly sensitive to light, making it easier to detect distant planets and even analyze their atmospheres. These missions will combine several techniques, including transit and direct imaging, to gather more information about exoplanets and to look for signs of life.

Some scientists are even working on "starshades," large spacecraft designed to block out a star's light from a great distance, allowing telescopes to take clearer pictures of exoplanets. Others are studying the possibility of detecting the light from biosignatures—chemicals in an exoplanet's atmosphere that could indicate the presence of life, like oxygen or methane.

The Question of Life

To understand the possibility of life on other worlds, scientists focus on what we know about life here. Earth is our only example so far, so we use it as a starting point. On Earth, we know that life needs a few things: liquid water, a source of energy, and certain chemical ingredients like carbon, hydrogen, nitrogen, and oxygen. That's why, when scientists search for signs of life on exoplanets, they look for clues that these conditions might exist there too.

The Role of Water in Life

Water is one of the most important ingredients for life as we know it. On Earth, every living thing—from the tiniest microbe to the largest whale—depends on water. Water allows chemicals to mix and react in ways that are essential for life, making it a kind of "universal solvent" where many vital processes take place.

Scientists believe that if we're going to find life on other planets, liquid water will likely need to be there too. This is why astronomers are so interested in finding exoplanets located in the "habitable zone," sometimes called the "Goldilocks zone." This is the region around a star where temperatures are just right for water to exist as a liquid. If a planet is too close to its star, it would be too hot, and water would boil away as vapor. If it's too far, it would be too cold, and any water would freeze into ice. But in the habitable zone, there's a chance that liquid water might exist on the planet's surface.

Not every planet in the habitable zone has water, and even if it does, that doesn't guarantee life. Still, the presence of liquid water makes a planet a more promising place to look. Some scientists even think that life could exist on planets or moons with subsurface oceans, like Jupiter's moon Europa, which is covered in ice but has a liquid ocean beneath it. This means that life might be able to thrive even in places without sunlight, as long as there's water and a source of energy.

Energy Sources: Powering Life

Another essential ingredient for life is energy. On Earth, most life forms get their energy either from the Sun, through photosynthesis, or from eating other organisms. However, some unique forms of life, called extremophiles, live in environments where sunlight can't reach. For example, deep under the ocean near hydrothermal vents, extremophiles survive by using chemicals released from the vents as an energy source. This has led scientists to believe that life could exist on other planets or moons even if there's no sunlight, as long as there's some other energy source available.

Finding planets that might have sources of energy isn't easy, but scientists can look for clues. For example, planets with active volcanoes, a magnetic field, or chemical reactions in their atmosphere might be able to support forms of life that rely on chemical energy instead of sunlight. In our search for life, scientists keep an open mind about what kinds of environments might provide the energy needed for life to thrive.

Building Blocks of Life: The Right Chemistry

Life on Earth is made from specific chemical building blocks, mainly carbon, hydrogen, oxygen, and nitrogen. These elements combine in various ways to form molecules like proteins, DNA, and sugars, which are essential for living things. When scientists search for signs of life, they look for planets with similar chemical ingredients.

One way scientists can detect these elements is by studying the atmospheres of exoplanets. When light from a planet's star passes through its atmosphere, some of the light gets absorbed by the gases present, creating a kind of "fingerprint." By studying this fingerprint, scientists can figure out which gases are in the atmosphere. If a planet's atmosphere contains oxygen or methane, for example, it could be a sign of life, as these gases are often produced by living organisms.

Still, scientists keep in mind that life elsewhere could be different. It's possible that alien life might use a different set of chemicals or might be based on something other than carbon, like silicon. While carbon is very versatile and forms the basis of life on Earth, there's always a chance that other elements could work in a different environment. Keeping an open mind helps scientists consider a wider range of possibilities.

Extremophiles: Life in Extreme Conditions

One of the biggest discoveries about life on Earth is that it can survive in extreme conditions. These organisms, known as extremophiles, live in places once thought too harsh for life. Some extremophiles thrive in boiling hot springs, while others live in the freezing ice of Antarctica. Some even survive in highly acidic or salty environments. Studying extremophiles has shown scientists that life can adapt to many types of conditions, which expands the kinds of exoplanets where we might look for life.

For example, scientists once thought that a planet would need to be warm and sunny to support life. But extremophiles have shown us that life might exist in places with little sunlight, extreme temperatures, or high radiation levels. This opens up the possibility of finding life on planets that don't seem "Earth-like" at all. If life can adapt to these extreme environments on Earth, perhaps it could also adapt to conditions on other planets.

Biosignatures: The Signs of Life

When scientists search for life on exoplanets, they look for "biosignatures," which are signs that life might be present. A biosignature could be a particular chemical in the atmosphere, a combination of gases, or even certain patterns in how light reflects off a planet. On Earth, for example, oxygen is a major biosignature because it's mostly produced by plants and algae through photosynthesis. If scientists find oxygen in an exoplanet's atmosphere, it could suggest the presence of life.

Another potential biosignature is methane, a gas that can be produced by living organisms. On Earth, methane is released by certain types of bacteria and also from decaying plants. If a planet has both oxygen and methane in its atmosphere, it's even more interesting because these gases don't normally coexist for long without life processes to produce them.

Biosignatures are exciting clues, but they aren't proof of life. Some processes, like volcanoes or chemical reactions in rocks, can also produce gases like methane and oxygen. That's why scientists study biosignatures carefully and look for patterns that can't be explained by non-living processes. The search for biosignatures is one of the reasons why new telescopes, like the James Webb Space Telescope, are being designed to analyze the atmospheres of distant exoplanets in greater detail.

The Search for Life Beyond Earth: What's Next?

The search for life on other planets is just beginning, and each new exoplanet discovery brings new possibilities. With advanced technology, scientists are exploring the atmospheres, climates, and compositions of distant worlds, hoping to find conditions that could support life. Space missions and telescopes will soon be able to analyze the light from exoplanets in even more detail, allowing us to search for biosignatures and other clues of life.

While we haven't found life on any exoplanet yet, the search is far from over. Each time scientists find a planet in the habitable zone or detect interesting chemicals in an atmosphere, the excitement grows. The question of whether we are alone in the universe drives astronomers to keep searching, exploring, and learning more about the conditions that could support life.

7

THE MYSTERIES OF SPACE

Black Holes

Black holes are some of the strangest and most mysterious objects in space. They're places where gravity is so strong that not even light can escape. Imagine a giant cosmic trap that pulls in everything that comes too close—planets, stars, gas, and even light. Once something crosses the "point of no return" around a black hole, it's gone forever. This point is called the event horizon, and anything that crosses it is pulled deeper and deeper into the black hole. But how do black holes form, and what makes them so powerful?

To understand black holes, we first need to understand what happens when a massive star reaches the end of its life. Stars are like gigantic factories of energy, powered by a process called nuclear fusion. Fusion happens when atoms smash together and produce huge amounts of energy, and this energy is what makes a star shine. Fusion also creates a lot of pressure that pushes outward, balancing the star's gravity, which is constantly trying to pull everything inward. For most of a star's life, there's a balance between this outward pressure from fusion and the inward pull of gravity, keeping the star stable.

But eventually, a massive star runs out of fuel, and fusion slows down. Without fusion to keep the star stable, gravity takes over, pulling everything inward with tremendous force. The core of the star collapses, and the outer layers explode in a supernova—a massive, bright explosion that can outshine an entire galaxy for a short time. What's left after the explosion depends on the mass of the star. If the core is big enough, it will collapse even further, creating a black hole.

What Makes a Black Hole So Strange?

A black hole isn't like a planet or a star. It doesn't have a surface that you can touch or stand on. Instead, it's more like a region of space where gravity is so strong that it warps space and time. This warping is caused by the incredible density of the black hole. When a massive star's core collapses into a black hole, it gets squeezed into a tiny space. Imagine squeezing something as big as the Sun down to the size of a city. This small, dense point at the center of a black hole is called a singularity, and it's where all the mass of the black hole is concentrated.

The closer you get to a black hole, the stronger its gravitational pull becomes. If you got too close, the gravity would stretch you out in a process scientists call "spaghettification." This is because gravity pulls harder on the parts of you that are closer to the black hole than on the parts that are farther away. If you're falling feet-first toward a black hole, your feet would be pulled harder than your head, stretching you out like spaghetti!

Once you cross the event horizon, you'd be pulled toward the singularity, where all of the black hole's mass is packed. No one knows exactly what happens inside the event horizon because nothing, not even light, can escape to tell us what it's like. This mystery makes black holes one of the most fascinating objects in the universe.

Types of Black Holes: Stellar, Supermassive, and Intermediate

Not all black holes are the same size. In fact, they can range from small to absolutely enormous. There are three main types of black holes: stellar black holes, supermassive black holes, and intermediate black holes.

Stellar black holes are the "smallest" type, although they're still huge compared to anything on Earth. These black holes form from the collapse of massive stars, like the one we just talked about. Stellar black holes usually have a mass between a few times and about 20 times that of the Sun. They're found scattered throughout galaxies, often in areas where massive stars have exploded in supernovas.

Supermassive black holes are much, much larger. These giants sit at the centers of galaxies, including our own Milky Way. Supermassive black holes can have masses millions or even billions of times that of the Sun. Scientists are still trying to understand how supermassive black holes form, but one idea is that they grew over billions of years by pulling in gas, stars, and other material. Our galaxy's center has a supermassive black hole called Sagittarius A*, and even though it's incredibly dense, it's about 4 million times the mass of our Sun.

There's also a type of black hole that's somewhat in between these two, called intermediate black holes. These black holes are thought to have masses between 100 and 10,000 times that of the Sun. They're harder to find because they're smaller than supermassive black holes and don't emit as much energy. Some scientists believe intermediate black holes could be the "building blocks" that eventually merge to form supermassive black holes.

How Do We Detect Black Holes?

Since black holes don't emit any light, you might wonder how scientists can even find them. The answer is that black holes reveal their presence by interacting with the matter around them. When a black hole pulls in gas and dust, this material forms a swirling disk called an accretion disk. The gas in this disk gets heated up to extremely high temperatures, producing X-rays and other forms of radiation that we can detect with telescopes.

Scientists also find black holes by observing how they affect nearby stars. If a star is orbiting something invisible but very massive, it could be a black hole. By studying the star's orbit, astronomers can calculate the mass of the object it's orbiting. If the object is massive enough to be a black hole but isn't emitting light, then we know it's likely a black hole.

Another way to detect black holes is through gravitational waves. When two black holes collide and merge, they create ripples in space-time called gravitational waves. These waves spread out across the universe, and sensitive detectors on Earth can pick them up. The first detection of gravitational waves in 2015 confirmed that black holes can merge, creating even larger black holes. Gravitational waves have opened up a whole new way of studying these mysterious objects.

What Happens Near a Black Hole?

The area around a black hole is a place of extreme forces and strange effects. For example, time slows down as you get closer to a black hole. This is because gravity affects time, a phenomenon explained by Albert Einstein's theory of general relativity. If you watched someone fall toward a black hole from a distance, it would look like they were moving in slow motion as they approached the event horizon. To them, time would seem normal, but to you, it would look like they were taking longer and longer to fall. In fact, at the event horizon, time seems to stand still.

Another strange effect near a black hole is the warping of space. Black holes bend the fabric of space, creating a kind of "well" around them. This bending is so extreme that if light passes close to a black hole, it gets curved around it. This effect, called gravitational lensing, allows astronomers to see multiple images of the same star or galaxy, as the light bends around the black hole's gravity. This lensing effect can even allow scientists to detect black holes by studying how they bend the light from distant objects.

The Mystery of the Singularity

At the heart of every black hole is a point where all the mass is concentrated into an infinitely small space. This point is called the singularity, and it's where the laws of physics break down. At the singularity, gravity becomes so strong that our understanding of how the universe works no longer applies. Scientists aren't exactly sure what happens at the singularity, and it's one of the biggest mysteries in modern physics.

Some scientists think that studying singularities could help us discover new physics that goes beyond what we know now. Others wonder if black holes might contain "wormholes" or tunnels that connect different parts of space and time. This idea, though purely theoretical, suggests that black holes could be gateways to other places in the universe, or even to other universes. While we don't have any evidence that this is true, the idea continues to capture the imagination of scientists and science fiction fans alike.

Black Holes and the Future of Space Exploration

Studying black holes isn't just about solving cosmic mysteries—it could also be important for the future of space exploration. Black holes hold the key to understanding gravity, space, and time at their most extreme. By studying them, scientists hope to learn more about the fundamental forces that shape our universe.

Black holes also inspire new technologies. The gravitational waves detected from colliding black holes have led to advancements in how we measure distances in space. Who knows? Future space missions might even be able to explore black holes up close, using technology we can only imagine today.

Dark Matter and Dark Energy

What exactly are dark matter and dark energy? The truth is, no one fully knows. They're two of the biggest mysteries in space, and scientists are still piecing together clues to understand them. But even though we can't see dark matter or dark energy, their effects are all around us, shaping the universe in ways that we can measure and observe.

Dark Matter: The Invisible Glue

Dark matter is something that scientists believe acts like an invisible "glue" holding galaxies together. To understand why scientists think it exists, let's look at how galaxies work. Galaxies are enormous collections of stars, dust, and gas that rotate around a center. According to what we know about gravity, the stars on the outer edges of galaxies should be moving more slowly than the stars closer to the center. But when scientists studied the motion of stars in galaxies, they found something strange—the stars at the edges were moving just as fast as the ones near the center. This didn't make sense based on what we know about gravity.

To explain this mystery, scientists proposed the idea of dark matter. They think there's an unseen substance in each galaxy, adding extra gravity and holding the galaxy together. Dark matter doesn't emit, absorb, or reflect light, which is why we can't see it. We know it's there only because of the way it affects the things we can see, like the stars and galaxies. Without dark matter, galaxies would fly apart because there wouldn't be enough gravity to keep them together.

But what is dark matter made of? That's another mystery. Scientists have some ideas, but so far, no one has detected dark matter directly. Some think it could be made of particles unlike anything we've ever encountered, particles that don't interact with regular matter in any way except through gravity. Experiments all over the world are trying to catch a glimpse of these particles, but so far, dark matter remains hidden.

Dark Energy: The Force Behind the Universe's Expansion

Dark energy is even stranger than dark matter. While dark matter is like a cosmic glue holding things together, dark energy seems to do the opposite—it's pushing the universe apart. To understand why dark energy is so mysterious, let's go back to the discovery that the universe is expanding.

In the early 20th century, scientists discovered that galaxies are moving away from each other, meaning that the universe is getting bigger. This was surprising, but scientists thought they had it mostly figured out. They believed that, although the universe was expanding, gravity would gradually slow it down over time, like a ball thrown into the air that eventually stops rising and falls back down.

But in 1998, something astonishing was discovered. When scientists studied very distant galaxies, they found that the universe's expansion wasn't slowing down—it was speeding up. This meant that something was pushing the universe apart, something stronger than gravity. That "something" was given the name dark energy. Dark energy is thought to make up about 70% of the universe, and it's the force driving the accelerated expansion.

What exactly is dark energy? No one knows for sure, but one idea is that it might be related to the "vacuum" of space itself. Even in areas of space that seem empty, there could be energy hidden in the vacuum, and this energy might have a repulsive effect, pushing galaxies away from each other. Other scientists think dark energy might be connected to something even more fundamental about space and time. But like dark matter, dark energy is a puzzle that scientists are still trying to understand.

How Do We Know Dark Matter and Dark Energy Exist?

If dark matter and dark energy are invisible, how do we know they exist? Scientists rely on evidence from the way they affect things we can see, like stars, galaxies, and even the universe itself. Let's look at some of the clues that have led scientists to believe in dark matter and dark energy.

One of the most important pieces of evidence for dark matter comes from galaxy clusters. A galaxy cluster is a group of galaxies held together by gravity. When scientists studied these clusters, they found that there wasn't enough visible matter to account for the amount of gravity holding them together. Something else, something invisible, had to be providing the extra gravity needed to keep the cluster intact. That something is thought to be dark matter.

Another clue about dark matter comes from gravitational lensing. This is a phenomenon where light from a distant galaxy is bent and distorted by the gravity of a massive object, like a galaxy or a galaxy cluster, lying in between. When scientists observe gravitational lensing, they often find that there isn't enough visible mass to create the effect they're seeing. This means there must be extra, unseen mass bending the light—again, likely dark matter.

For dark energy, the evidence comes from observing the rate of the universe's expansion. Scientists use certain types of stars, called supernovae, as "standard candles" to measure distances in space. When they looked at very distant supernovae, they found that these galaxies were farther away than expected if the universe's expansion were slowing down. This suggested that the universe's expansion is actually speeding up, which led to the idea of dark energy.

The Cosmic Microwave Background (CMB), which is the faint glow left over from the Big Bang, also provides clues about dark matter and dark energy. By studying patterns in the CMB, scientists can get a snapshot of the early universe and see how matter was distributed. These patterns tell us that there's much more matter in the universe than what we can see, suggesting the presence of dark matter, and they also support the idea that dark energy is driving the universe's accelerated expansion.

The Hunt for Dark Matter and Dark Energy

Scientists are constantly working to learn more about dark matter and dark energy, and there are many experiments and telescopes focused on these mysteries. One type of experiment is designed to catch particles of dark matter directly. These experiments are often located deep underground, where they're protected from cosmic rays and other sources of interference. Scientists hope that, by creating very sensitive detectors, they'll be able to catch a dark matter particle interacting with regular matter.

Another approach is to study dark matter and dark energy indirectly through large telescopes that observe galaxies and galaxy clusters. The Vera C. Rubin Observatory, which is currently under construction, will create detailed maps of the sky, helping scientists study the effects of dark matter and dark energy on a massive scale. By mapping out how galaxies are distributed and how they're moving, scientists can gather more clues about how these mysterious forces shape the universe.

The European Space Agency is also launching a telescope called Euclid, which is specifically designed to study dark matter and dark energy. Euclid will observe billions of galaxies to help scientists understand how the universe's structure has changed over time. This information could provide new insights into the nature of dark energy and the role of dark matter in shaping galaxies.

Why Understanding Dark Matter and Dark Energy Matters

Understanding dark matter and dark energy isn't just about solving cosmic mysteries; it's about understanding the universe itself. Dark matter affects how galaxies form, how stars are distributed, and how the universe looks on a large scale. Without dark matter, our Milky Way galaxy wouldn't look the way it does. Dark energy, on the other hand, is changing the very fate of the universe. If dark energy continues to push the universe apart, galaxies will eventually move so far away from each other that future generations of astronomers won't be able to see them. The universe could become a cold, empty place with galaxies too far apart to interact.

8

BECOMING AN ASTRONOMER
OBSERVATIONAL ASTRONOMERS: THE WATCHERS OF THE SKY

Observational astronomers are like detectives with a telescope. They spend their time gathering data from space by observing celestial objects like stars, planets, galaxies, and nebulae. These astronomers often work at observatories, using powerful telescopes to capture images and collect light from distant objects. By analyzing this light, they can learn about the properties of these objects, such as their temperature, composition, distance, and motion.

Observational astronomers don't always work with optical telescopes—the kind that collects visible light. Space also gives off other types of radiation, like radio waves, infrared light, X-rays, and gamma rays. Some observational astronomers specialize in "radio astronomy," using giant radio telescopes to pick up radio waves from space. Others might work with X-ray or infrared telescopes to study objects that emit those types of light, revealing things we couldn't see with just visible light. Each kind of light tells astronomers something different, so observational astronomers are always expanding our understanding of the universe by looking at it in new ways.

Theoretical Astronomers: The Thinkers and Calculators

Theoretical astronomers are like the planners and thinkers of astronomy. They don't usually work with telescopes or observe space directly. Instead, they use mathematics, physics, and computer models to understand how the universe works. Imagine trying to figure out how a galaxy forms, how black holes behave, or what the conditions were like right after the Big Bang. These are the types of questions theoretical astronomers explore.

By creating simulations on computers, theoretical astronomers can model things like star formation, the movement of galaxies, and even the behavior of dark matter. These models help them predict what might happen under certain conditions. When observational astronomers make new discoveries, theoretical astronomers use these findings to adjust their models and theories, refining our understanding of space. In this way, observational and theoretical astronomers work hand in hand, each helping to explain what the other discovers.

Planetary Astronomers: Explorers of Our Solar System

Planetary astronomers focus on planets, moons, and other objects within our solar system, and sometimes even exoplanets (planets orbiting stars outside our solar system). They study everything from the rocky surface of Mars to the icy moons of Jupiter to the comets and asteroids that zip through space. Planetary astronomers try to answer questions like: How did our solar system form? What are the conditions on other planets? Could there be life elsewhere?

Some planetary astronomers work with data from spacecraft that visit other planets. For example, the rovers on Mars, the Juno mission around Jupiter, and the New Horizons mission that flew by Pluto have all provided incredible data for planetary astronomers to study. These scientists analyze the images and measurements sent back by these missions, searching for clues about the composition, history, and potential habitability of other worlds.

Planetary astronomers also study exoplanets, especially ones that could be similar to Earth. They look for planets in other star systems that are in the "habitable zone," where conditions might allow for liquid water. By studying these distant worlds, planetary astronomers hope to find planets that might support life, adding new pieces to the puzzle of whether we are alone in the universe.

Stellar Astronomers: The Life Cycle of Stars

Stars are at the center of stellar astronomers' work. These scientists study everything about stars, from how they're born in massive clouds of gas and dust to how they burn brightly for millions or billions of years, and finally, how they die in explosive supernovas or as gentle, cooling white dwarfs. Stars are constantly changing, and by studying them, stellar astronomers learn more about the processes that power the universe.

One of the biggest questions for stellar astronomers is understanding the life cycle of stars. Different types of stars have different life spans and end in different ways. For instance, massive stars may end in a supernova explosion, leaving behind a neutron star or a black hole, while smaller stars like our Sun eventually turn into white dwarfs. By studying star clusters, star-forming regions, and individual stars, stellar astronomers piece together the story of how stars evolve.

Stellar astronomers are also interested in variable stars, which are stars that change in brightness over time. By tracking these changes, they can learn about the star's temperature, size, and even the presence of other objects nearby, like planets or companion stars. Studying stars can help astronomers understand how galaxies are built and how they change over time, since stars are the main components of galaxies.

Galactic Astronomers: Studying the Vastness of Galaxies

Galactic astronomers focus on the huge, star-filled islands we call galaxies. Our galaxy, the Milky Way, contains hundreds of billions of stars, along with gas, dust, and dark matter. But the Milky Way is just one of billions of galaxies in the universe, and each one has its own unique structure, composition, and history. Galactic astronomers study these massive structures to learn how they formed and how they evolve.

Galaxies come in different shapes and sizes—spiral, elliptical, and irregular—and galactic astronomers try to understand why. By studying galaxies, they can learn about the role of dark matter, the way stars are distributed, and how galaxies interact with each other. For example, some galaxies collide and merge, forming even larger galaxies. Studying these interactions helps astronomers understand the structure of the universe on a large scale.

One exciting area of galactic astronomy is the study of supermassive black holes at the centers of galaxies. These enormous black holes can influence the movement of stars and even the shape of their galaxies. By studying galaxies and their central black holes, galactic astronomers are uncovering new details about the forces that shape the cosmos.

Cosmologists: The Scientists of the Universe's Origins

Cosmologists study the universe as a whole, focusing on its origins, structure, and ultimate fate. They ask big questions, like: How did the universe begin? What is it made of? How will it end? Cosmologists study things like the Big Bang, dark matter, and dark energy, trying to understand how these forces affect the universe. They use both observational data and theoretical models to explore these mysteries.

One of the biggest mysteries in cosmology is dark energy, the force causing the universe to expand at an accelerating rate. Another mystery is dark matter, which doesn't emit light but seems to hold galaxies together. Cosmologists study the distribution of galaxies and use observations of the cosmic microwave background (the faint glow left over from the Big Bang) to learn more about these unknown substances.

Cosmology is one of the most challenging and fascinating fields in astronomy because it tackles questions that are almost impossible to answer. But every discovery, every new observation, brings us closer to understanding the nature of the universe.

Astrobiologists: The Search for Life Beyond Earth

Astrobiology combines astronomy and biology to explore one of the most intriguing questions of all: Is there life beyond Earth? Astrobiologists study the conditions that make life possible and look for clues about where life might exist elsewhere in the universe. They work with planetary astronomers, chemists, and biologists to understand the types of environments that could support life.

Astrobiologists examine extreme environments on

Earth, like deep-sea vents and hot springs, where "extremophiles" (organisms that can survive in extreme conditions) live. By studying these organisms, astrobiologists learn more about the kinds of life that might survive in harsh environments on other planets or moons. They're particularly interested in places like Mars, the icy moon Europa, and even exoplanets that might have liquid water.

The discovery of even the simplest life form on another planet would be one of the greatest scientific discoveries ever. Astrobiologists are helping us explore that possibility, searching for clues about life's origins and potential beyond our planet.

Space Instrumentation Specialists: The Engineers of Astronomy

While they might not study space directly, space instrumentation specialists are essential to the field of astronomy. They design and build the instruments that make astronomical discoveries possible, like telescopes, cameras, and detectors. These scientists and engineers work on the technology that allows astronomers to see farther and in more detail than ever before.

Space instrumentation specialists work on projects like the Hubble Space Telescope, the James Webb Space Telescope, and the Mars rovers. They design instruments that can operate in extreme environments, collecting data and sending it back to Earth. Their work makes it possible for observational astronomers to gather the data that leads to new discoveries. Without them, we wouldn't have the amazing images and detailed information that have transformed our understanding of the universe.

Skills Needed: Curiosity, math, and science.

Curiosity: The Fuel for Every Astronomer's Journey

Curiosity is one of the most important traits for any scientist, and it's especially important for astronomers. Astronomy is all about asking questions: How did the universe begin? Are there other planets like Earth? What happens inside a black hole? These questions are the starting points for many astronomers, sparking their desire to learn more about the cosmos.

Curiosity isn't just about asking questions, though; it's about having the drive to find answers. Many of the mysteries that astronomers study can take years—or even decades—to solve. Imagine spending years researching the same galaxy, or analyzing data to understand one star's unusual behavior. Without curiosity, it would be hard to keep going. Curiosity pushes astronomers to keep exploring, even when the answers aren't easy to find.

Astronomers often don't find the answers right away, and sometimes the answers lead to even more questions. For example, scientists once thought the universe was just filled with stars and galaxies. Then they discovered dark matter and dark energy, which opened up whole new mysteries. Each discovery in astronomy often brings a new layer of questions, which means curiosity is never-ending in this field.

Math: The Language of the Universe

If you're dreaming of becoming an astronomer, math is one of the most important skills you'll need. Math is like a language that astronomers use to describe everything they observe. It helps them understand the size of stars, the distance between galaxies, and even the movement of planets. Without math, it would be nearly impossible to make sense of all the data that astronomers collect.

One of the first math skills astronomers use is geometry. Geometry helps them measure distances and angles, both of which are essential in astronomy. Imagine looking at a star through a telescope and trying to figure out how far away it is. By measuring the angles and using geometry, astronomers can calculate distances that are billions of light-years away. Geometry is also used to understand orbits, helping astronomers predict how planets and moons move around each other.

Algebra is another important part of an astronomer's toolkit. Algebra allows astronomers to solve equations that describe how stars change over time or how galaxies move in relation to each other. Algebra helps astronomers track changes and understand patterns in space, which is essential for studying objects that are too far away to reach.

Astronomy also requires calculus, a type of math that deals with change and motion. Calculus is used to understand how things in space interact with each other. For instance, when scientists study the orbits of planets or the motion of galaxies, calculus helps them predict these movements and understand the forces involved. It's also used to understand how light from distant stars and galaxies changes as it travels to Earth.

Statistics is another key area in astronomy. Astronomers often work with huge amounts of data, whether it's from telescopes, satellites, or computer simulations. Statistics helps them analyze this data, find patterns, and draw conclusions. For example, if an astronomer is studying thousands of stars, statistics can help them identify trends in brightness, color, and temperature. Statistics is essential for sorting through data and making sense of what astronomers see.

Science: The Foundation of Astronomy

Astronomy is a science, and like all sciences, it's built on a foundation of scientific principles. To understand the universe, astronomers need a solid understanding of physics, chemistry, and sometimes even biology. Each of these sciences gives astronomers the tools to understand different parts of the universe.

Physics is the backbone of astronomy. Everything in space follows the laws of physics, from the way stars shine to the movement of galaxies. Physics explains how gravity pulls planets into orbits, why stars form in giant clouds of gas, and how black holes trap light. In fact, much of what we know about space comes from applying physics to observations. For example, by understanding how gravity works, astronomers can predict how planets will move and how galaxies will interact. Physics helps explain the forces at play in the universe and gives astronomers a framework for studying objects that are too far away to touch or see up close.

One area of physics that is especially important in astronomy is optics, the study of light. Since astronomers observe objects by studying the light they emit, knowing how light behaves is crucial. Optics helps astronomers understand how telescopes work and how light travels through space. By understanding optics, astronomers can create better telescopes and find new ways to study the universe.

Chemistry is also an important tool in astronomy, especially for studying the composition of stars, planets, and other celestial objects. By analyzing the light that objects emit, astronomers can figure out what elements are present. For example, the Sun emits light that contains certain wavelengths, or colors, and each wavelength corresponds to a specific element. By studying these wavelengths, astronomers can tell that the Sun contains hydrogen, helium, and small amounts of other elements. This technique, called spectroscopy, helps astronomers determine what stars and planets are made of, even though they're light-years away.

Some astronomers, especially those interested in finding life beyond Earth, also study biology. While we haven't found life elsewhere in the universe, understanding the conditions needed for life can guide astronomers in their search. This field, called astrobiology, combines knowledge of biology and astronomy to explore questions about life in the cosmos. By studying life on Earth, especially in extreme environments like deep-sea vents or frozen deserts, astrobiologists can guess what types of conditions might support life on other planets.

Problem-Solving Skills: Tackling the Unknown

Astronomy often involves working with the unknown, which means that astronomers need to be excellent problem-solvers. They deal with questions that don't have clear answers and often face challenges that require creativity to solve. Imagine trying to study a galaxy millions of light-years away, knowing that you'll never be able to visit it in person. Instead, astronomers have to find indirect ways to learn about it, using telescopes, data, and models.

One way astronomers approach problems is by breaking them down into smaller questions. For example, if they want to understand how a star forms, they might start by studying the clouds of gas and dust where stars begin. They might then look at how gravity pulls these clouds together, and finally, how nuclear fusion starts in the core of a new star. By tackling each part of the process, they can start to understand the bigger picture.

Astronomers also need patience and perseverance. Space is vast, and answers often come slowly. An astronomer might spend years studying the same object, collecting data over long periods and piecing together clues. When studying stars or galaxies, it often takes time to gather enough information to make a discovery. This means that astronomers need to be persistent, willing to work through setbacks, and ready to keep going even when progress is slow.

Communication: Sharing Discoveries with the World

Astronomers don't just make discoveries—they also share their findings with the world. Communication is a crucial skill for astronomers, whether it's writing research papers, giving presentations, or talking to the public. Astronomy is a global field, with scientists from all over the world working together and sharing data, so being able to explain ideas clearly and effectively is essential.

Astronomers often work in teams, collaborating with other scientists, engineers, and technicians. Good communication helps these teams work together smoothly, especially when they're tackling complex problems. An astronomer might need to explain their findings to colleagues who work in different fields or communicate their discoveries to people who don't have a background in science. By sharing their work, astronomers can inspire others, raise new questions, and help expand our understanding of the universe.

Communicating about astronomy isn't always easy, especially when it involves complex topics like dark matter, black holes, or the expansion of the universe. But when astronomers take the time to explain their discoveries, they make space more accessible and inspire future generations to keep exploring.

Fun Ways to Learn More

Stargazing Clubs: Exploring the Night Sky Together

If you've ever looked up at the stars and wondered what's out there, stargazing clubs are a fantastic way to dive deeper into that curiosity. These clubs are groups of people who come together to observe the sky, share knowledge, and learn from each other. Many stargazing clubs have telescopes you can use, so even if you don't have your own, you can still experience close-up views of planets, the Moon, and sometimes even distant galaxies.

In a stargazing club, you might meet amateur astronomers who have been observing the sky for years. They can help you find constellations, spot planets, and recognize other celestial objects. Many of them love to share tips on how to observe, what to look for, and even how to set up a telescope. Stargazing clubs often meet at places away from city lights, where the sky is darker and it's easier to see faint stars. This is called "dark sky" observing, and it's one of the best ways to see details in the night sky that might be hidden by light pollution in cities.

Stargazing clubs also host special events during exciting astronomical occurrences, like meteor showers, lunar eclipses, or when a planet is especially visible. Joining one of these events can be thrilling because you get to see something that doesn't happen every night. Being around others who share your interest makes it even more fun, and you'll learn a lot from the experienced members.

Science Museums and Planetariums: Windows to the Cosmos

Science museums and planetariums are like gateways to the universe. Many science museums have entire sections dedicated to space and astronomy, with exhibits that let you explore everything from the planets in our solar system to the mysteries of black holes. You might find hands-on activities where you can build a model rocket, create a map of the stars, or even see what it's like to be in a spacesuit.

Planetariums are special theaters where the ceiling is like a giant, curved screen that shows the night sky. Using powerful projectors, planetariums can simulate what the sky looks like on a clear night, even if it's daytime or cloudy outside. You can see constellations, planets, and even distant galaxies, all from the comfort of a theater seat. Many planetariums offer shows that take you on a journey through space, exploring everything from the birth of stars to the far reaches of the cosmos. It's like taking a mini trip through the universe without ever leaving Earth.

At science museums, you might also find displays about space missions, with real objects that astronauts have used, like pieces of spacesuits, parts of rockets, or models of spacecraft. These exhibits help you learn about the challenges of space travel and the incredible technology that makes it possible. Some science museums even have simulators where you can experience what it feels like to be an astronaut, adding a bit of adventure to your visit!

Astronomy Books and Magazines: Knowledge at Your Fingertips

Books and magazines are fantastic resources for learning about space on your own time. There are books written just for young astronomers, filled with pictures, fun facts, and activities. Some of these books cover the basics of astronomy, teaching you about stars, planets, and galaxies. Others might focus on specific topics like black holes, the search for exoplanets, or famous space missions.

Astronomy magazines are another great way to keep up with the latest discoveries. Many magazines are packed with stunning images from space telescopes like Hubble or the James Webb Space Telescope, along with articles explaining what these discoveries mean. They also have sky charts that show you what you can see in the sky each month, making it easy to plan your own stargazing adventures.

Some popular astronomy magazines, like *Sky & Telescope* or *Astronomy*, often include sections just for beginners. They might have tips for stargazing, reviews of telescopes, and even projects you can try at home. It's exciting to flip through the pages and see the latest in space exploration, and magazines often introduce you to new topics and questions you may not have thought of yet.

Online Resources and Apps: Space Exploration from Your Device

Thanks to technology, you can explore the universe right from your computer or tablet. Many websites and apps are designed to help young astronomers learn more about space and even do their own observing. Websites like NASA's official site or the European Space Agency's site have sections specifically for kids, with games, quizzes, videos, and activities.

One of the coolest things about astronomy apps is that they often include "sky maps." These maps show you what the night sky looks like in real time. You can point your device at the sky, and the app will label stars, planets, and constellations, making it easy to know what you're looking at. Apps like SkySafari, Star Walk, or Stellarium are popular among stargazers, and they're like having a mini planetarium in your pocket.

Some online resources even let you join live broadcasts of astronomical events. For example, when there's a lunar eclipse or a special planetary alignment, organizations like NASA or observatories around the world will stream the event. This means you can watch it from anywhere, even if the sky is cloudy where you are. Many of these events include experts explaining what's happening, so you can learn while you watch.

Astronomy Camps and Programs: Learning While Having Fun

Imagine spending a week in the summer surrounded by other kids who are just as excited about space as you are. Astronomy camps are special programs where you can do hands-on activities, go stargazing, and learn from real astronomers. Some astronomy camps even take place in remote areas with very dark skies, giving you a perfect view of the stars.

At astronomy camps, you might get the chance to use high-powered telescopes, learn how to take pictures of the night sky, and participate in activities that teach you about planets, stars, and other objects in space. Many camps have guest speakers who are astronomers, scientists, or even astronauts, giving you the chance to learn from people who study space for a living.

If you're interested in more intense programs, some universities and observatories offer summer programs for young astronomers. These programs might include things like building your own telescope, doing mini research projects, or using real data from space telescopes to study stars or galaxies. These types of experiences can be inspiring, giving you a taste of what it's like to work in astronomy and encouraging you to keep exploring.

Observing Challenges and Projects: Practice Makes Perfect

If you enjoy stargazing, try setting up some challenges or projects for yourself. For example, you might try to spot every planet visible in the night sky over a month or map out the constellations you can see from your home. Another fun project is to keep a stargazing journal. Each time you observe the night sky, write down what you saw, where you were, and anything interesting you noticed. Over time, you'll start to notice patterns, like when certain constellations are visible or how the position of the planets changes.

Some young astronomers enjoy learning how to do basic astrophotography, which is taking pictures of the night sky. You don't need fancy equipment to get started; even a smartphone can capture bright objects like the Moon or some planets. Learning to photograph the sky teaches you patience and helps you understand the details of what you're observing.

Another idea is to follow the phases of the Moon for a month, observing how it changes shape night by night. Understanding the Moon's cycle will make it easier to plan future observations, and it's exciting to see how it waxes, wanes, and moves through its different phases.

Star Parties: Celebrating the Night Sky with Others

Star parties are gatherings where people come together to observe the sky, usually organized by stargazing clubs, science museums, or observatories. They're often held in places with very dark skies, far from city lights, which means you'll get a clearer view of stars, planets, and other celestial objects. Star parties can be big events, with hundreds of people, or small gatherings where a few people bring their telescopes and share the night.

At a star party, you'll have the chance to look through different types of telescopes, each with its own way of revealing the wonders of space. You might see Jupiter's cloud bands, Saturn's rings, or distant star clusters. Experienced astronomers are usually there to guide you, pointing out interesting objects and explaining what you're seeing. Star parties are a great way to meet people who share your interest, and it's exciting to discover new objects together under a star-filled sky.

9
THE FUTURE OF SPACE EXPLORATION

Space tourism is all about making space travel possible for everyday people. Companies are designing rockets, spacecraft, and other systems to give people a chance to see Earth from space, experience zero gravity, and get a view that only a handful of astronauts have ever seen. It's a thrilling time for space exploration, and it's exciting to think that trips to space might become as common as airplane flights in the future.

Space Tourism: How Did We Get Here?

For decades, space travel was something only governments could afford. The United States, Russia, and later other countries like China and Japan, launched astronauts into space using rockets funded by national space agencies, like NASA. But over time, private companies became interested in space. These companies began to imagine a future where space travel wasn't limited to astronauts on government missions. They wanted to make space accessible to ordinary people and find ways to make it safe, enjoyable, and—eventually—affordable.

The first hints of space tourism began with a few wealthy individuals who were able to pay millions of dollars to go into space. In 2001, American businessman Dennis Tito became the first "space tourist" when he paid around $20 million to travel to the International Space Station (ISS) on a Russian spacecraft. This journey inspired other companies to start developing ways to make space tourism more accessible to more people.

Today, companies like SpaceX, Blue Origin, and Virgin Galactic are all working hard to bring space travel closer to reality. Each company has a different approach, but they all have the same goal: to give people a chance to experience space.

Virgin Galactic: A Ride to the Edge of Space

Virgin Galactic is one of the first companies to start selling tickets for space tourism. Founded by British entrepreneur Sir Richard Branson, Virgin Galactic focuses on "suborbital" space flights. This means that the spacecraft goes up to the edge of space but doesn't complete a full orbit around Earth. Even though it doesn't go all the way around the planet, it still reaches an altitude where passengers can see the blackness of space and experience a few minutes of weightlessness.

Virgin Galactic's spacecraft, called VSS Unity, is

launched from a large airplane. The airplane, known as the mothership, carries the spacecraft to high altitude, where it releases VSS Unity. The spacecraft's rocket engines then ignite, propelling it into the upper atmosphere and giving passengers a view of Earth from the edge of space. After a few minutes of weightlessness, the spacecraft glides back down to Earth and lands like a regular plane.

For those brief moments in space, passengers get to float around, look out the windows at the curve of Earth, and experience what it's like to be in zero gravity. Virgin Galactic aims to make space tourism available to as many people as possible, and they've already sold hundreds of tickets to future passengers. Right now, the tickets are still very expensive, but the company hopes to bring the price down over time, making it more accessible to more people.

Blue Origin: Going Up with New Shepard

Blue Origin is another company leading the way in space tourism. Founded by Jeff Bezos, the founder of Amazon, Blue Origin has developed a rocket called New Shepard. Unlike Virgin Galactic's approach, New Shepard is a fully reusable rocket designed for vertical launches and landings. This means it takes off from a launch pad, reaches the edge of space, and then comes back down, landing upright.

New Shepard takes passengers on a suborbital trip, similar to Virgin Galactic's flights, reaching the edge of space where they can experience weightlessness. The rocket has a capsule with large windows, giving passengers an incredible view of Earth and the blackness of space. During the trip, passengers float around the cabin, taking in the view and enjoying the feeling of being weightless. After a few minutes, the capsule begins its descent back to Earth, landing gently with the help of parachutes.

In 2021, Blue Origin made history by flying Jeff Bezos himself, along with three other passengers, including the oldest and youngest people ever to go to space. Blue Origin's goal is to make these trips a regular occurrence, allowing more people to experience space travel without having to spend years in astronaut training.

SpaceX: Orbiting the Earth and Beyond

SpaceX is perhaps the most ambitious company in space tourism, aiming to take passengers not just to the edge of space, but all the way into orbit. Founded by Elon Musk, SpaceX has been a leader in reusable rocket technology, which is helping make space travel more affordable and sustainable. SpaceX's rocket, Falcon 9, and its spacecraft, Dragon, have already been used to send astronauts to the International Space Station.

In 2021, SpaceX made history with a mission called Inspiration4, which was the first all-civilian mission to orbit Earth. This means that none of the passengers were professional astronauts—they were ordinary people who trained for the mission. The crew spent three days orbiting Earth, experiencing life in space, and conducting science experiments. They even had a special observation dome installed in the Dragon spacecraft, giving them a 360-degree view of space.

SpaceX's plans for the future include more orbital missions, as well as potential trips around the Moon. The company is developing a new spacecraft called Starship, which is designed for long-distance space travel. Elon Musk has even talked about the possibility of taking people to Mars someday. While this might be a long way off, SpaceX is pushing the boundaries of what's possible in space tourism.

What It's Like to Be a Space Tourist

Space tourism offers a new kind of adventure, but it's different from any other type of travel. Going to space requires training, and passengers have to be in good health. Most space tourists take part in a few days of training, learning about the spacecraft, practicing safety procedures, and preparing for the effects of zero gravity. While the training isn't as intense as what astronauts go through, it helps prepare passengers for what they'll experience.

One of the most exciting parts of space tourism is experiencing weightlessness. When the spacecraft reaches a certain altitude, passengers start to float as if they were underwater. This happens because they're in free-fall, moving at the same speed as the spacecraft, which creates the feeling of zero gravity. Space tourists can float around the cabin, do somersaults, and even pour water into the air to watch it float in droplets.

Looking out the window is another unforgettable part of the experience. Space tourists get to see Earth from a new perspective, with the bright blue oceans, green land, and swirling clouds below. Many astronauts say that seeing Earth from space is life-changing because it shows how fragile and beautiful our planet is. Space tourists will have the chance to experience this view and understand why space exploration is so important.

The Future of Space Tourism: Making Space Accessible

As space tourism companies keep improving their technology and lowering costs, more people will have the chance to experience space. Right now, only a few people can afford a ticket, but companies like Virgin Galactic, Blue Origin, and SpaceX are working to make it more affordable over time. Some experts believe that within a few decades, space tourism might be as common as taking a vacation on an airplane.

In the future, we might even see space hotels, where people can stay in orbit for longer periods. Imagine spending a few days on a space station, looking out the window at Earth every morning. Space hotels would allow people to experience life in space, complete with zero gravity, views of the universe, and the thrill of orbiting Earth. Companies like Axiom Space are already working on plans to build private space stations that could one day host tourists, scientists, and even filmmakers.

Colonizing Mars

Why Mars? The Search for a New Home

Mars is about half the size of Earth, and it's the fourth planet from the Sun. Although it's very different from Earth, it shares some interesting similarities. A day on Mars, called a sol, is only slightly longer than a day on Earth—about 24.6 hours. Mars also has seasons, polar ice caps, and a variety of landscapes, including mountains, valleys, and deserts. These features make it the most Earth-like planet in the solar system.

But there are big differences too. Mars is much colder than Earth, with an average temperature of minus 80 degrees Fahrenheit, which is colder than Antarctica. Its atmosphere is very thin, containing mostly carbon dioxide with almost no oxygen, making it impossible to breathe. Water, a necessity for life, exists only as ice or in small amounts beneath the surface. These challenges mean that if humans want to live on Mars, they'll need to bring a lot of equipment with them or find ways to use the resources available on Mars.

Despite these challenges, scientists believe that Mars could be a potential "second home" for humanity. The idea is that if we learn how to live on Mars, we could continue exploring and perhaps even settle on other planets in the future. Learning to live on Mars could be the first step toward becoming a "multi-planetary" species.

Building Habitats: Homes on Mars

One of the biggest challenges of living on Mars is creating safe habitats, or homes, for people to live in. Since Mars doesn't have breathable air or comfortable temperatures, habitats would need to be carefully designed to keep people safe and healthy. These habitats would need to be airtight to protect from the thin, carbon dioxide-filled atmosphere, and they would have to be well-insulated to keep out the extreme cold.

Scientists and engineers have come up with many creative ideas for building habitats on Mars. Some propose using materials found on Mars, like Martian soil, to construct buildings. This technique, called "in-situ resource utilization," would reduce the amount of material we'd need to bring from Earth. Martian soil could be mixed with water to make a kind of concrete or 3D-printed to create walls. Using local materials would save money and make the colonies more self-sufficient.

Other ideas involve habitats built underground or in caves. Underground habitats would be protected from radiation, which is a big problem on Mars because it doesn't have a strong magnetic field to shield it from the Sun's harmful rays. Building habitats underground could keep people safe from radiation while also providing stable temperatures.

For the inside of these habitats, scientists would need to create a livable environment with air, heating, and lighting. Oxygen generators would be essential to produce breathable air, and heaters would help keep the temperature comfortable. Some habitats might have gardens to grow fresh food and recycle carbon dioxide into oxygen, helping create a mini-Earth environment on Mars.

The Importance of Water: Finding and Using Mars' Water Resources

Water is one of the most critical resources for any human settlement, and it's something that would be challenging to find on Mars. While there's no liquid water on Mars' surface, scientists know there's ice in certain areas and likely small amounts of water trapped in the soil. Figuring out how to access and use this water would be essential for any colony.

One idea for getting water on Mars is to extract it from the ice caps at the planet's poles. The poles are covered with ice made mostly of carbon dioxide, but there's also water ice mixed in. Melting this ice would provide water for drinking, growing plants, and even making fuel. Another possibility is to "mine" the water trapped beneath the surface. Special drills could be used to dig for frozen water in Martian soil, which would then be melted and purified.

Water on Mars could also be used to create oxygen

and rocket fuel. By separating water into hydrogen and oxygen, scientists could produce breathable air and fuel for rockets, which would be important for any future Mars missions. This process, called electrolysis, would allow humans to make use of Mars' resources rather than relying entirely on supplies from Earth.

Food for Martian Settlers: Growing Crops on the Red Planet

Food is another major challenge for a Mars colony. Shipping large amounts of food from Earth would be expensive and impractical for a long-term colony, so scientists are exploring ways to grow food on Mars. The idea of farming on Mars is complicated because Martian soil lacks the nutrients that plants need to grow. It also contains a substance called perchlorate, which is toxic to humans. Before any food can be grown, scientists would need to find a way to treat or clean the soil.

One possible solution is to use hydroponics, a method of growing plants without soil. In a hydroponic system, plants grow in water enriched with nutrients, which could be created using the materials available on Mars. This method doesn't require soil, which would make it easier to grow crops in the controlled environment of a Martian habitat. Hydroponic gardens could provide fresh vegetables and fruits, which would be a vital source of nutrition for settlers.

Scientists are also testing crops that might be able

to grow in Martian soil with some adjustments. Experiments on Earth have shown that certain plants, like potatoes and certain grains, can grow in soil similar to that found on Mars. If these crops could be grown on Mars, it would mean that settlers could produce their own food and become more self-sufficient, reducing the need for supplies from Earth.

Energy Sources: Powering a Martian Colony

For any colony to thrive on Mars, it would need a reliable source of energy. Without energy, there would be no heat, no oxygen production, and no way to grow food or communicate with Earth. Solar power is one option for energy on Mars because the planet receives sunlight, although not as much as Earth. Solar panels could be set up to capture sunlight and convert it into electricity. However, Mars also has dust storms that can block sunlight for days or even weeks, so relying solely on solar power could be risky.

Nuclear energy is another option that scientists are considering. Nuclear reactors could provide a steady source of power regardless of weather conditions. NASA has been working on small, portable nuclear reactors called Kilopower, which could be used to power habitats, vehicles, and other equipment on Mars. These reactors are designed to be safe and efficient, providing power even during dust storms.

Wind power is a less likely option because Mars' atmosphere is much thinner than Earth's, meaning the winds don't carry as much energy. However, if scientists find that wind turbines could work on Mars, they might use them as a backup source of power.

The First Steps: Preparing for a Journey to Mars

Establishing a colony on Mars would be one of the biggest challenges humanity has ever faced, and it would require careful planning and preparation. Before any humans can live on Mars, scientists need to send robotic missions to gather information and test equipment. Rovers like NASA's Perseverance are already exploring Mars, collecting samples, and searching for signs of ancient life. These missions help scientists understand the planet's environment and test technologies that might be used for future human missions.

NASA and other space agencies are also working on testing life-support systems, habitats, and spacesuits. Scientists even conduct experiments in places on Earth that are similar to Mars, like deserts and frozen regions, to practice what life might be like for Mars settlers. Astronauts train in simulated Mars habitats to learn how to live and work in the harsh conditions they would face on Mars.

Companies like SpaceX have announced plans to send people to Mars within the next decade, using powerful rockets designed for long-distance space travel. The goal is to eventually build a self-sustaining colony on Mars, where humans could live independently from Earth. This vision of a Martian colony is ambitious, and it will likely take many years to accomplish, but each new mission brings us closer to that goal.

Why Mars Matters: Exploring New Frontiers

Exploring Mars isn't just about finding a new place to live; it's about understanding more about our own planet and the potential for life elsewhere. Studying Mars can teach us about the history of the solar system, how planets form, and what conditions are necessary for life. By learning to live on Mars, we might also find new ways to solve problems on Earth, like how to grow food in extreme conditions or generate power with limited resources.

You in Astronomy

Asking Big Questions: Curiosity and Discovery

Curiosity is the heart of science, and in astronomy, it's one of the most important qualities to have. The universe is vast and filled with mysteries, and every great discovery starts with a question. Right now, scientists are wondering about things like how the universe began, what dark matter is, and whether there's life beyond Earth. But there are plenty of other questions that haven't even been asked yet, and you might be the one to think of them.

Some of the biggest breakthroughs in astronomy came from people asking unusual questions. For example, astronomer Vera Rubin wondered why galaxies spin the way they do, which led to the discovery of dark matter. Questions like "What would it take to live on Mars?" or "Could there be liquid oceans under the ice on distant moons?" have sparked entire fields of research. Your questions about the universe could be just as important. As you grow, keep asking questions about things you're curious about, because those questions could inspire future discoveries.

Learning Science and Math: Building Your Space Skills

Astronomy combines many different subjects, especially science and math, and learning these subjects can help prepare you for a future in space exploration. Right now, things like algebra or physics might seem challenging, but they're the tools astronomers use to understand everything from the orbits of planets to the behavior of stars. Math and science are like the languages of the universe, and learning them opens up a whole new way of seeing the world.

Physics, for example, helps explain the forces that keep planets in orbit, make stars shine, and power rockets. Chemistry helps scientists understand the makeup of stars, planets, and even distant galaxies. And don't forget about technology—knowing how to use computers and coding can be incredibly useful in astronomy. Many astronomers use computer simulations to model how galaxies form, how black holes behave, or even how life might survive in extreme environments.

If you're interested in space, there are lots of ways to start building your skills. You could try experimenting with a telescope, doing science experiments at home, or learning about coding through online resources. These activities help you understand the tools astronomers use and give you a head start on the skills you'll need for the future.

Contributing to Space Science Right Now

Believe it or not, there are ways kids and young people can actually contribute to space science right now. There are projects called "citizen science" projects, which invite anyone—kids included—to help scientists with research. These projects often need people to look at images from telescopes, listen for signals, or report what they see in the night sky. By participating, you can help scientists find new stars, track asteroids, or even discover new exoplanets.

One popular citizen science project is called Zooniverse, which has a range of different projects, including some related to space. For example, in the project Planet Hunters, people look at data from the Kepler Space Telescope to help identify possible new planets around distant stars. Another project, Galaxy Zoo, asks volunteers to look at images of galaxies and help classify their shapes. These projects are open to anyone, and they're a great way to learn about space science while making a real contribution.

Other organizations, like NASA and the European Space Agency, also have programs for young people. NASA's "Be a Martian" program invites people to help analyze images from Mars rovers. And SETI (Search for Extraterrestrial Intelligence) allows people to help listen for signals from space that could indicate other life forms. These projects let you participate in space exploration from your computer at home, bringing you one step closer to the stars.

Inventing the Future: Creativity and Innovation

Astronomy and space exploration are fields that depend on creativity just as much as knowledge. To explore space, scientists and engineers often have to think outside the box and come up with new solutions to big problems. When we sent rovers to Mars, for example, engineers had to design a way for them to survive in an extremely harsh environment, move around on rocky terrain, and send data back to Earth.

One of the big challenges in space exploration today is finding ways to protect astronauts from radiation, which is much stronger in space than on Earth. Another challenge is creating habitats that allow people to live comfortably on other planets, like Mars. These challenges require creative solutions, and that's where you come in. You could be the person who invents the technology that makes space travel safer or builds the equipment that allows us to explore planets more easily.

If you like to invent things or come up with ideas,

think about how your creativity could help solve the problems of space travel. You could start by designing models, experimenting with simple science projects, or even just writing down ideas about how to solve challenges in space exploration. Remember, every big invention starts with a single idea.

Thinking Like a Scientist: Problem Solving

Space exploration isn't easy, and one of the most important skills for anyone interested in astronomy is problem-solving. Scientists and engineers face unexpected problems all the time, whether it's a spacecraft malfunctioning or a rocket launch being delayed. To be successful in space science, you need to learn how to approach problems, test solutions, and think creatively.

Let's say you want to explore a distant moon covered in ice, like Europa. You'd need to figure out how to get there, how to land safely, and how to drill through the ice to see what's underneath. Each step of the way would require problem-solving. The same goes for finding ways to grow food in space or building systems to recycle water and air on long missions.

You can practice problem-solving in everyday life by working on puzzles, playing games that require strategy, or tackling challenges in science and math. Each time you solve a problem, you're training your brain to think like a scientist. And someday, those skills might help you solve some of the biggest challenges in space exploration.

Getting Involved in Astronomy: School and Community

Even at a young age, there are lots of ways to start learning more about space and getting involved in astronomy. You could join a science club at school, find a local astronomy club, or participate in stargazing events in your community. Some schools even have programs where you can learn to build model rockets or learn about space technology.

If your school doesn't have an astronomy club, maybe you could start one! You could organize meetings where people watch videos about space, talk about recent discoveries, or plan trips to a nearby planetarium. Clubs are a great way to share your interest with others and to learn from each other. You might even inspire your friends to get interested in space, too.

Museums and science centers often have exhibits and activities related to space, and many of them host special events where you can meet astronomers and ask questions. Planetariums, which are theaters that show the night sky on a dome-shaped screen, are also great places to learn about astronomy and see what the universe looks like up close.

Dreaming Big: You and the Future of Space

Right now, people all over the world are working on incredible projects in space exploration. Some are studying Mars, while others are planning missions to explore the icy moons of Jupiter and Saturn. Others are working on telescopes that can look deeper into the universe than ever before, searching for signs of other planets and life beyond Earth. The scientists, engineers, and astronauts leading these projects were once kids with big dreams, just like you.

One day, it might be your turn to explore the stars, and the journey starts with the things you're curious about right now. Whether it's building rockets, discovering new planets, or solving mysteries about the universe, your future in astronomy is wide open. As you keep learning and exploring, remember that the skills you're building today could help shape the next great adventure in space exploration. You could be the one who makes history, discovering things about the universe that no one has ever seen before. And who knows? The next chapter in space exploration might have your name on it.

GLOSSARY OF ASTRONOMY TERMS
ASTEROID

Asteroids are small, rocky objects that orbit the Sun, mostly found in a region called the asteroid belt between Mars and Jupiter. They're like space rocks, ranging in size from tiny pebbles to objects that are hundreds of miles across. Unlike planets, asteroids are too small to be round and don't have atmospheres.

Astronomer

An astronomer is a scientist who studies space, stars, planets, and everything beyond Earth's atmosphere. Astronomers use telescopes, computers, and sometimes even spacecraft to learn about the universe. They ask big questions about how stars are born, what black holes are, and whether there might be life beyond Earth.

Atmosphere

An atmosphere is a layer of gases that surrounds a planet, star, or moon. Earth's atmosphere, for example, is a mix of nitrogen, oxygen, and other gases that protect us from the Sun's harmful rays and help us breathe. Not every planet has an atmosphere, and some, like Mars, have very thin ones.

Black Hole

A black hole is a region in space with gravity so strong that nothing, not even light, can escape from it. Black holes form when very massive stars collapse at the end of their life cycle. Scientists believe there are black holes at the center of most galaxies, including our own, the Milky Way.

Comet

Comets are icy objects that orbit the Sun. When a comet gets close to the Sun, its ice starts to melt, forming a glowing cloud and a tail that streams away from the Sun. Comets come from far-off regions of the solar system, and their tails can stretch for millions of miles.

Constellation

A constellation is a group of stars that forms a pattern in the sky. People have named constellations after animals, mythological characters, and everyday objects for thousands of years. Some famous constellations include Orion (the Hunter) and Ursa Major (the Big Bear).

Dark Matter

Dark matter is a mysterious substance that makes up most of the matter in the universe. Scientists can't see dark matter, but they know it exists because of the way it affects the movement of galaxies. Unlike normal matter, dark matter doesn't emit light, which is why it's called "dark."

Exoplanet

An exoplanet is a planet that orbits a star outside our solar system. Scientists have discovered thousands of exoplanets, and some of them might even have conditions that could support life. Exoplanets come in many sizes and types, some even larger than Jupiter or smaller than Earth.

Galaxy

A galaxy is a massive system of stars, planets, gas, dust, and dark matter, all held together by gravity. Our solar system is in the Milky Way galaxy, which contains hundreds of billions of stars. Galaxies come in different shapes, like spiral, elliptical, and irregular.

Gravity

Gravity is a force that pulls objects toward each other. It's what keeps us on Earth and what keeps the planets orbiting the Sun. Gravity depends on the mass of an object and the distance between objects, meaning larger objects like stars have stronger gravity.

Light-Year

A light-year is the distance that light travels in one year, about 5.88 trillion miles. It's used to measure extremely large distances in space, like the distance between stars or galaxies. For example, the nearest star to us, Proxima Centauri, is about 4.24 light-years away.

Meteor

A meteor is a piece of space debris, usually from an asteroid or a comet, that burns up when it enters Earth's atmosphere. This creates a streak of light in the sky, often called a "shooting star." If part of a meteor survives its journey through the atmosphere and reaches the ground, it's called a meteorite.

Nebula

A nebula is a giant cloud of gas and dust in space. Nebulas are often the birthplaces of stars, as gravity pulls the gas and dust together to form new stars. Some famous nebulas include the Orion Nebula and the Eagle Nebula.

Orbit

An orbit is the path an object takes around another object in space. For example, Earth orbits the Sun, and the Moon orbits Earth. Orbits are usually elliptical (oval-shaped), and they're the result of gravity pulling objects together.

Planet

A planet is a large object that orbits a star and doesn't produce its own light. In our solar system, there are eight planets, including Earth. Planets are divided into two groups: rocky planets (like Earth and Mars) and gas giants (like Jupiter and Saturn).

Pulsar

A pulsar is a type of neutron star that emits beams of radiation from its poles. As it spins, these beams sweep across space, creating a pulsing effect like a cosmic lighthouse. Pulsars are formed when massive stars collapse, and their strong magnetic fields make them fascinating to study.

Red Giant

A red giant is a type of star that has used up most of its fuel. As a star ages and runs out of hydrogen to burn, it expands and cools, becoming a red giant. Eventually, red giants shed their outer layers, leaving behind a dense core that can become a white dwarf.

Rocket

A rocket is a vehicle designed to travel through space. Rockets carry fuel that burns to create thrust, allowing them to overcome Earth's gravity and reach space. Rockets are used to launch satellites, astronauts, and other equipment into orbit and beyond.

Satellite

A satellite is any object that orbits a larger object. There are natural satellites, like moons, and artificial satellites, which are man-made objects launched into space. Satellites are used for communication, weather forecasting, GPS, and scientific research.

Solar System

A solar system is made up of a star and all the objects that orbit it, including planets, moons, asteroids, and comets. Our solar system includes the Sun, eight planets, and many smaller objects. Solar systems can vary greatly and are found throughout the universe.

Spacecraft

A spacecraft is a vehicle designed to travel in space.

Unlike rockets, which are mainly used for launching, spacecraft can carry out missions, such as exploring planets or collecting data from space. Examples of spacecraft include the Mars rovers and the Voyager probes.

Star

A star is a massive ball of hot gas, mostly hydrogen and helium, that produces light and heat through nuclear fusion. The Sun is a star, and there are billions of other stars in our galaxy. Stars vary in size, color, and brightness, and they have life cycles from birth to death.

Supernova

A supernova is a powerful explosion that happens when a massive star runs out of fuel and collapses. This explosion releases an enormous amount of energy, creating bright light that can outshine an entire galaxy for a short time. Supernovas spread heavy elements into space, which helps form new stars and planets.

Telescope

A telescope is an instrument that helps us see objects that are far away. There are many types of telescopes, including optical telescopes, which collect visible light, and radio telescopes, which collect radio waves. Telescopes make it possible to study planets, stars, and galaxies in detail.

Universe

The universe is everything that exists: all of space,

time, matter, and energy. It includes galaxies, stars, planets, black holes, dark matter, and dark energy. The universe is constantly expanding, and scientists believe it began with a big event called the Big Bang.

White Dwarf

A white dwarf is the dense core left behind after a red giant star sheds its outer layers. It's very small and extremely hot, but it doesn't produce new energy. White dwarfs gradually cool over time and represent one of the final stages in a star's life.

RESOURCES
WEBSITES FOR SPACE EXPLORERS

1. NASA Kids' Club

NASA's Kids' Club is a fun and interactive site where you can learn about space missions, play games, and watch videos about different topics in astronomy. It's designed for young explorers and has a ton of information straight from NASA, making it a great place to start if you're interested in space missions and the work astronauts do.

2. ESA Kids (European Space Agency)

ESA Kids offers games, videos, and activities focused on space exploration. The site is packed with cool features, including information about Europe's space missions, robots exploring Mars, and what it takes to be an astronaut. There's also a section on how to spot constellations, perfect for budding astronomers.

3. Zooniverse

Zooniverse is a citizen science website where people from all over the world help scientists with real research. They have projects where you can look at images of galaxies, help identify stars, and even search for exoplanets. It's a unique way to learn about space while actually contributing to science.

4. Stellarium Web

Stellarium Web is an online planetarium that lets you explore the night sky from your computer. You can search for constellations, planets, and stars, and it shows you what the sky looks like at any time and from any location. It's perfect for planning a stargazing night and learning how to find objects in the sky.

5. Space Place by NASA

Space Place is another excellent resource from NASA, designed for younger audiences. It covers a variety of topics, from black holes to the Moon, and has interactive features, like quizzes and games. The explanations are simple and fun, making it easy to understand even complex topics.

6. SETI@home

SETI@home is a program that lets people use their computers to help search for extraterrestrial signals. By running this program, you can help scientists analyze radio signals from space. It's an exciting way to get involved in the search for life beyond Earth, even from your own home.

Apps for Stargazing and Space Exploration

1. Star Walk 2

Star Walk 2 is a stargazing app that shows you the night sky in real time. Point your phone or tablet at the sky, and the app will label stars, planets, and constellations. It also includes information about celestial events like meteor showers and eclipses, making it perfect for planning your stargazing adventures.

2. SkyView Lite

SkyView Lite is another fantastic stargazing app that helps you explore the sky. It shows the positions of stars, planets, and constellations, and includes fun facts about each object. It even has an augmented reality mode, where you can see labels and information overlaid on the real night sky.

3. NASA App

The official NASA app is a must-have for space enthusiasts. It's packed with news about space missions, photos, and videos from NASA, as well as information about planets, stars, and galaxies. You can even track the location of the International Space Station (ISS) in real time.

4. ISS Detector

ISS Detector is an app that lets you know when the International Space Station will be passing over your location. It's a simple app, but it's incredibly cool to be able to spot the ISS moving across the sky. The app also shows you the best times for viewing satellites and other objects in orbit.

5. Solar Walk

Solar Walk is a 3D model of the solar system that

lets you explore planets, moons, and other objects. You can zoom in on each planet, learn facts about them, and watch how they orbit the Sun. It's an interactive way to learn about our solar system and see everything up close.

6. Universe in a Nutshell

Based on the popular book by astrophysicist Neil deGrasse Tyson, this app lets you explore the scale of the universe. You can zoom in and out to see objects from the tiniest atom to the largest galaxies, all in one app. It's a great way to understand just how big (and small) everything in the universe really is.

Fun Space Activities and Experiments to Try

1. Build a Model Solar System

Use household items like balls, paper, or clay to create your own model of the solar system. Arrange the planets in order from the Sun and see how they vary in size and distance. It's a fun way to learn about the planets and how they orbit the Sun.

2. Make a Constellation Viewer

Create your own constellation viewer with a cardboard tube, paper, and a flashlight. Punch tiny holes in the paper in the shape of a constellation, then shine a flashlight through it to project the constellation onto a wall. This activity helps you learn about constellations and how to recognize them in the sky.

3. Create a Moon Journal

Track the phases of the Moon for a month. Each night, look at the Moon and draw what you see, or write down its shape. By the end of the month, you'll have a complete picture of the Moon's cycle and a better understanding of how it changes over time.

4. Explore Shadows and the Sun

Place a stick or pencil in the ground and observe how its shadow changes throughout the day. This experiment helps you understand how the Earth's rotation affects the position of the Sun in the sky and how shadows move because of it.

5. Meteor Shower Watch

Check for upcoming meteor showers using an app or website like Space Place. Plan a night to go outside, lay down on a blanket, and watch the meteors streak across the sky. Meteor showers are exciting events that happen when Earth passes through debris from a comet.

Milton Keynes UK
Ingram Content Group UK Ltd.
UKHW020027271124
451585UK00014B/1505